U CN
SPL BTR

U CN
SPL BTR

Spelling Tips for
Life Beyond Texting

■ ■ ■

DR. LAURIE E. ROZAKIS

CITADEL PRESS
Kensington Publishing Corp.
www.kensingtonbooks.com

To Raul the Pool Boy

CITADEL PRESS BOOKS are published by

Kensington Publishing Corp.
119 West 40th Street
New York, NY 10018

Copyright © 2008 Laurie E. Rozakis

Previously published in a hardcover edition under the title *"I" Before "E" Except After "C"*.

All Kensington titles, imprints, and distributed lines are available at special quantity discounts for bulk purchases for sales promotions, premiums, fund-raising, educational, or institutional use. Special book excerpts or customized printings can also be created to fit specific needs. For details, write or phone the office of the Kensington special sales manager: Kensington Publishing Corp., 119 West 40th Street, New York, NY 10018, attn: Special Sales Department; phone 1-800-221-2647.

CITADEL PRESS and the Citadel logo are Reg. U.S. Pat. & TM Off.

First trade paperback printing: September 2009

10 9 8 7 6 5 4 3 2 1

Printed in the United States of America

Library of Congress Control Number (hardcover edition): 2008922841

ISBN-13: 978-0-8065-2885-4
ISBN-10: 0-8065-2885-0

Contents

■ ■ ■

Introduction

■ ■ ■

Dear ~~Reeder~~, ~~Reder~~, Reader,

At one time or another, we're all bothered by balky vowel movements. Indeed, some of us are plagued by them. Ah, but you're a resourceful person, so you try to cure these distressing issues with *a, e, i, o, u* (and sometimes *y*) on your own.

First, you always run a computerized spell-check on every document you write. That's a great idea. After all, it's a perfectly logical place to start. And you do cure the most obvious problems, such as switched or missing letters. Nonetheless, you still are tripped up by easily confused word pairs and word triples such as *their/they're/there*. And you can't always run a computerized spell-check because you're often called on to write something the old-fashioned way—with a pen or pencil. That's a real problem.

So what can you do next? Maybe you learn some spelling rules. Brilliant! Now you're able to catch even more mistakes, but—the rules don't always work. For instance, perhaps you recite your new mantra "I before e except after c" every time you write a word with the "ie" or "ei" pattern. That's all well and good until you encounter some exceptions, such as *leisure, weird,* and *seize.* Aarrgg. By now, you're getting a little frustrated. Perhaps you mutter in your discomfort, "What am I doing wrong that causes me to have so much trouble with spelling?"

It's not your fault; really it's not. It's English. Our glorious language is rich and vibrant and all that stuff, but it's also riddled with words that are challenging to spell. *U Cn Spl Btr* can't regularize English spelling—no one can do that—but it *can* provide you with an easy and effective way to become a better speller. And you'll have a great time learning.

In chapter 1, I explain why spelling matters and how poor spelling can hold you back on the job and in your personal life. In chapter 2, you'll learn how English got so screwed up: you'll discover that you can blame a lot of it on the Great Vowel Shift rather than your seventh-grade teacher, Mr. Jerk. Chapter 3 covers why people misspell words; chapter 4, how to learn to spell. In chapters 5 through 8, I'll take you gently step-by-step through phonics, the real word for vowel movements. Chapter 9 focuses on adding letters before and after root words, while chapter 10 explores spelling rules (only the ones that work, of course). Chapter 11 zeroes in on spelling contractions and plurals. In chapter 12 you get the pot of gold, heaps of spelling demons.

So take my hand and let me lead you to the land of cooperative vowel movements. It's a place of leafy green trees, unending happy hours, and good spelling.

Acknowledgments

■ ■ ■

Despite the name on the cover, a book is always a collaborative effort. First, my deep thanks to my editor Gary Goldstein, international man of mystery, who possesses a great sense of history and humor. Second, a tip of the hat to production editor Arthur Maisel for his attention to detail. I'd also like to acknowledge copyeditor Bonnie Fredman, and the proofreader, a key player in a spelling book.

Chapter 1

Why Spelling Matters

■ ■ ■

Three men arrive at the gates of heaven. First, we have Butch, a car mechanic respected for his honesty. Then we have Garrett, a brain surgeon celebrated for his compassion. Last, we have George, a lawyer known for, well, being a cutthroat lawyer.

St. Peter greets them: "Welcome to Heaven. We have simplified the process of admission, so now to get into Heaven all you need do is pass a one-word spelling test. Are you ready?"

Butch says, "I've prepared for this moment for seventy-eight years. I'm all set."

"Let's begin," St. Peter intones in a deep voice. "Spell *car*."

Butch grins and says, "C-a-r."

St. Peter smiles and says, "Excellent, Butch. Welcome to heaven."

Addressing St. Peter, Garrett the brain surgeon says, "I'll take my test now, if it pleases you."

"Here's your test," St. Peter intones in his deep voice. "Spell *love*."

The former doctor grins and says, "L-o-v-e."

St. Peter smiles and says, "Excellent, Garrett. Welcome to heaven." Then St. Peter turns to George, the lawyer. George is muttering to himself, "Boy, this is gonna be a walk in the park. Who would have thought it? I'm sure ready to turn the table on all those lawyer jokes." George turns to St. Peter and says, "Give me my test."

"Okay," St. Peter says. "Spell *prorhipidoglossomorpha.*"

Hey, you never know when those spelling skills will come in handy.

Thomas Jefferson knew a great deal, which is why we name so many schools after him. He even knew the importance of spelling, saying, "Take care that you never spell a word wrong. Always before you write a word, consider how it is spelled. And if you do not remember, turn to a dictionary. It produces great praise to spell well." Indeed it does.

Dumb and Dumber (or Is That *Dum* and *Dummer?*)

Someone in serious spelling denial sent me this e-mail. (He really did. I couldn't make this up, even really late at night.):

Many peeple are abel to perform their jobs well even though there spelling is atrocous. I have never expereinced a problem because of my spelling in a vareity of jobs. I suppose some jobs are closed off to me, but for that matter many jobs are closed off for other reesons, such as the fact that I cannot do caluclus, I know nothing about banking, and I do not speak Urdu. Perhaps an inubility to spell would have had more sereush consequences before spell checkers became ubikuitous. Nowadays spelling is about as usefull as knowing how to shoe a horse. Thank you.

My answer:

No, thank <u>you</u>, dear writer. Please continue feeling this way. It helps keep editors and copyeditors employed. It also opens up a lot of jobs for those of us who <u>can</u> spell even if we can't do calculus, know nothing about banking, and don't speak Urdu.

Tragically for the world but fortunately for those of you who have bought this book and will soon be accomplished spellers, my anonymous e-mail buddy isn't the only one afflicted by poor vowel movements. As a result of e-mail, text messaging, Blackberrys, the decline of reading, poor teaching, and of course rock 'n' roll, a staggering number of people can't spell. Spell-checkers are useless because poor spellers often can't distinguish correct from incorrect words. (Besides, cell phones and Blackberrys don't come with spell-checkers.)

Just as a spot on your tie or a stain on your pants can destroy the good impression you're trying to make in person, so can a spelling error destroy the good impression you're trying to make in writing. What happens when a letter/e-mail/term paper/résumé has a whole lot of spelling errors? The writer comes across as a dolt.

Buying this book is your first step to curing poor vowel movements.

How Bad *Are* Your Vowel Movements?

Before we go any further, let's test your spelling health. The following chart has twelve often-mangled words. I chose these words because they're extremely common and useful, so much so that I'll bet you use at least one of them in school or on the job every day.

In the first column, I've listed a misspelled word. In the second and third columns, I have two different spellings for each word. Circle the correct spelling.

	Misspelled Word	Possible Correct Spelling	Possible Correct Spelling
1.	managment	managemant	management
2.	throuhout	thruout	throughout
3.	goverment	govrnment	government
4.	acommodate	acomodate	accommodate
5.	chocalate	chocolit	chocolate
6.	enviroment	enviranment	environment
7.	responsability	responsebility	responsibility
8.	recieve	receve	receive
9.	Febuary	Febrary	February
10.	occured	ocured	occurred
11.	officail	offical	official
12.	definately	definitily	definitely

Answers: In each case, the word in the third column is spelled correctly.

Full Disclosure

Time for a true confession: I, too, was afflicted with balky vowel movements. In my youth, I was a bad speller—a really bad speller. Even as late as high school, I mangled any word with an *ie,* never sure when *i* came before *e*. To make matters worse, I even argued with my beleaguered English teacher: if *i* really came before *e,* how can you explain *neither, either, weird,* and *leisure?* Of course I could never tell *weather* from *whether, witch* from *which,* and *stationary* from *stationery.* And what's with *their/they're/there?* You certainly didn't want to get me started on words that entered English from foreign languages. Their spelling never made any sense at all.

Eventually I learned the error of my ways and stopped railing against the injustices of ridiculous English spelling. Instead, I simply learned to spell. As a result, I was able to become an English teacher and lead others to the Light so that they, too, could distinguish *witch* from *which.*

Next time you're channel surfing for a ferocious, cut-throat sport, tune into the Scripps National Spelling Bee, the nation's largest and most famous bee. At the current time, around three hundred smarty-pants kids aged ten to fifteen make the finals. Looking for an even wilder and wackier weekend? Why not learn all the words on the Scripps National Spelling Bee list? You can download the word list from www.spelling bee.com/studyaids.shtml. Knock yourself out.

Spelling = Success

So why does spelling mastery matter so much? After all, none of us plans to win the National Spelling Bee for correctly spelling the twenty-five syllable word that identifies an extinct Australian marsupial, poisonous flowering plant, or chronic sinus condition. Yet spelling *really does* matter. Here are my top five reasons why.

Reason #1: Poor Spelling Can Damage Your Reputation

In 2006, actress Lindsay Lohan decided to send an e-mail to the world via her Blackberry, sharing her ideas for achieving world peace. Now, no one confuses Lohan with Einstein—or even with the rocket scientists among us who can spell both "bagel" and "bialy"—but her missive was stunning in its rambling incoherence. Furthermore, the letter's abysmal spelling astonished even those used to the ill-educated and overhyped media **boldfaced names.** Lohan's sloppy e-mail damaged her reputation.

Flash back to June 15, 1992. You surely remember how Dan Quayle became a laughingstock for "correcting" a student's spelling of "potato" as "potatoe" at an elementary school spelling bee in Trenton, New Jersey. Poor spelling suggests to people that you're ill-educated, careless, and lazy. And you are none of those.

Reason #2: Poor Spelling Holds You Back in School

Thanks to the nation's testing mania (which I like to call "No Child Left Untested" rather than "No Child Left Behind"), children are being barraged with a nonstop volley of standardized tests. From kindergarten to graduate school, students are subjected to an unprecedented number of high-stakes tests.

The outcome of these tests can have a significant impact on Little Johnny's or Little Janie's future. Did you bomb the writing part of the yearly state assessment? You're like to be forced to sweat through summer school or even to be denied entry to the next grade. Did you score poorly on the verbal part of the SAT? No hallowed ivy-covered college walls for you. Did you misspell a few crucial words on your Graduate Record Exam, Praxis Test, or any other state licensing exam? The scorer can deny you accreditation. "Any paper seriously deficient in the conventions of English" can result in its failure, according to the guidelines given to those of us who score the writing portions of national exams. And a chunk of those "conventions of English" refers to spelling.

What's the number one reason why articles are rejected for publication? Not their content, political bias, or writing style—it's their spelling and grammar errors.

Reason #3: Poor Spelling Holds You Back on the Job

Solid scholarly studies have shown that accomplished spellers read and speak with greater assurance than those who have not mastered spelling. The logic is unassailable: people who have mastered the mother tongue get ahead faster on the job than those who misuse and mangle the language. That's because people who use language with assurance have greater credibility. They're perceived as more intelligent.

An employee's credibility is based on the degree to which the perceiver finds the individual to be trustworthy and competent in the given topic area. When you're communicating through writing, the recipient can't judge your appearance, vocal quality, and body language. All the recipient has are your words on the page. Poor spelling damages your credibility—no matter how much you may know about the topic.

Reason #4: Good Spelling Enables You to Read and Think More Clearly

When you can spell well, you can recognize words correctly, figure out unfamiliar words, understand more of what you read, and retain more. Learning to spell well helps you form connections between word parts too. This helps you read more quickly. The better you read, the better you think.

Reason #5: Good Spelling Enables You to Write with Precision

Our language is a hearty stew simmered with words contributed from the Greeks, the Latins, the Angles, the Saxons, the Klingons, and many other people, some of whom appeared to have had deep-seated cooking issues. But that's the stew we've got, folks.

To say exactly what you mean, you need the exact word that states your meaning. Knowing how to spell many words gives you many choices, so you can use the word you need—not its first cousin.

Here are some examples:

What They Wrote	What They Meant
I recently bought this book from the estate of a *deceived* person.	I recently bought this book from the estate of a *deceased* person.
The county is holding a *pubic* meeting on Tuesday in town hall.	The county is holding a *public* meeting on Tuesday in town hall.
Nick broke his *humorous* bone.	Nick broke his *humerus* bone.

Furthermore, all words have *denotations*, their dictionary meaning. Many words also have *connotations*, subtle emotional overtones. You want to choose the words that have both the denotations and the connotations you want. You don't want to be forced to use an imprecise word because you can't spell the precise one. Try it now. Sort the following words according to their positive and negative connotations.

Words for **thin:** *lean, slender, scrawny, trim, lanky, gaunt, anorexic, willowy, emaciated, slim, frail, malnourished.*

Words with a Positive Connotation	Words with a Negative Connotation
_____	_____
_____	_____
_____	_____
_____	_____
_____	_____
_____	_____

Answers

lean	scrawny
slender	gaunt
trim	emaciated
willowy	frail
slim	anorexic
lanky	malnourished

"Spelling counts. Spelling is not merely a tedious exercise in a fourth-grade classroom. Spelling is one of the outward and visible marks of a disciplined mind." — *James J. Kilpatrick*

Cut to the Chase

Being a good speller marks you as a person of accomplishment, sophistication, and smarts.

Chapter 2

So How Did English Spelling Get So Screwed Up?

■ ■ ■

So for years you've been grousing, "English spelling is a *&%#*$ mess. It doesn't follow the rules." Your significant other mutters back, "Quit your kvetching. You can learn to spell if you want." Wait. You're both right. English spelling *is* quite a disaster, but you *can* learn to spell. Later in this book, I'll teach you some spelling rules and many other easy ways to beat the system. But—we're dealing with English spelling, so many of the rules have exceptions. Check out the following famous one:

How do you spell *fish?* *F-i-s-h* you say. Not so fast; it's also spelled *ghotti.* Here's how: Take the

gh in *tough*
o in *women*
ti in *action*

and you get *ghotti* (or *fish,* as it's also spelled).

How is this possible? It's possible because English has forty elementary sounds that you write with twenty-six letters.

Pssssssst—between you and me, English spelling has more quirks than the lady down the block who owns fifty-five cats. But relax. You'll discover that mastering English spelling is much easier when you understand its history. So sit back; get a (German) beer, some (French) fries, and an order of (Chinese) takeout; and relax while I take you on a brief history of the English language. At the end of our trip around the world, you'll understand why English spelling is like the boys in the cheap seats at the baseball stadium who keep dumping beer on our heads.

The Welcome (Word) Wagon

"Give me your tired, your poor, your huddled masses yearning to be free," Emma Lazarus wrote in a poem that was later engraved on the base of the Statue of Liberty. She was probably thinking more of welcoming people than she was of welcoming words, but with one came the other. (As well as a lot of tasty restaurant takeout and that fake French accent that's great for cheesy pickup lines.)

English is the most democratic and unrestricted language that ever existed. We have welcomed into our language words from scores of other languages and dialects, near and far, ancient and modern. And when we can't find a word that we need, we just invent one to fit the bill. Here's how the story starts.

"Honey, Did You Invite the Huns?"

For ages, fair-haired hunky sailors from North Germany roamed the high seas at will. Not a terribly discerning lot, these so-called Angles, Saxons, and Jutes aimed their beaked Viking ships at any country that promised booty. Around AD 449, the Anglo-Saxon mariners sailed across the North Sea and landed in a place they called Britannia. They liked the countryside, so they decided to conquer the people and set up camp. That's your mini-Masterpiece Theater version of how the Anglo-Saxons came to be the ancestors of English. It also explains why English is a Germanic language at heart.

The hundred most often used words in English all come from the Anglo-Saxons—as do eighty-three of the next hundred words.

Ye Olde English

Today we call the Anglo-Saxon language Old English. It was a nice language and served the people's needs just fine, thank you very much, until 1066 when the Normans came to England with an army headed by William, Duke of Normandy. William and his soldiers spoke French. Harold Saxon, England's head honcho, tried to fight off William and his army, but failed. Since the Normans had no intention of learning Old English (the Saxon language), they pressed their language on the masses. Hence, French became the official tongue. (Latin was used in church and school.) That's not to say that everyone suddenly stopped speaking Old English and started speaking French; actually, those stubborn peasants and their descendants kept right on chattering in Old English for another three hundred years. In effect, William's victory added a new layer of language as well as a new government and some decent food.

Ye Olde Middle English

After the Normans arrived on England's rocky shores, England was invaded repeatedly by cultures rather than warriors. As the English traded with their neighbors on the continent, they acquired words as well as goods. It took about three hundred years for Old English to become Middle English, and another three hundred years for Middle English to become Modern English.

The Big Daddy of Vowel Movements: The Great Vowel Shift

As if English spelling wasn't fluid enough in the fourteenth and fifteenth centuries, along came a change in the pronunciation of long vowels, the so-called Great Vowel Shift. This is the tsunami of vowel movements—the King Kong of vowel movements. The Great Vowel Shift changed the pronunciation of many English words and, hence, their spelling (not that the spelling had been carved in granite in the first place). The Great Vowel Shift is the dividing line between Middle English and Modern English.

Before the Great Vowel Shift, long vowels were pronounced like Latin vowels. During and after the Great Vowel Shift, the two highest long vowels became *diph-*

thongs and the other five were pronounced at a higher part of the tongue. A diphthong is one vowel with two sounds. Here are some examples:

Diphthongs	Examples
aw	paw
au	faucet
ou	mouse
ew	screw
oi	oil
oy	boy
ow	owl
ow	bow (a gathered ribbon on a package)
oo	moon
ŏŏ	cook
ai	lair
ee	leer

So how did pronunciation change during the Great Vowel Shift? For instance:

- The "i" in *mice* was originally pronounced like the "ee" in *feet,* so our long-ago ancestors said *meece* instead of *mice.*
- The "o" in *mouse* was originally like the "oo" in *moose,* so people said *moose* for *mouse.*

Naturally, since we're talking about English, the Great Vowel Shift wasn't uniform, so some English speakers today still pronounce some words as they were pronounced six centuries ago. You can find these dialects in Scotland. So the next time you're visiting the Loch Ness monster, listen to the locals chattering away to discover what Middle English sounded like.

No one knows why the Great Vowel Shift took place, but of course theories abound. Some people attribute it to the mass migration to southeast England as people fled the plague, but you can just as easily blame it on the bossa nova, alien abduction, or Elvis. Regardless of the cause, because English spelling was just becoming standardized in the 1400s and 1500s, the Great Vowel Shift gets the blame for many of the headaches of English spelling.

Spelling Gets Even More Fickle

Zipping through the years, around 1607, the Pilgrims, Puritans, and planters started hightailing it out of Europe, heading for our free and sunny shores. As early as 1621, Governor William Bradford and his fellow settlers in Plymouth Plantation were chatting up the Native Americans. Very quickly, American English became enriched with words from Native American dialects. Here are just a few words that we swiped from the Indians: *hickory, raccoon, possum, squash, pow-wow, chipmunk, moose, terrapin, quahog, hominy, pemmican*, and *moccasin*. More than twenty-five U.S. states—from Massachusetts to the Dakotas—have Indian names. Tricky to spell, these Native American words.

The words came with wave after wave of immigration. Our words traveled to American English in different ways—originally from ships and steerage and then on the *Concorde* and the *QE2*. Some of the richest sources of words came with immigrants from France, Spain, Italy, Germany, Poland, and Ireland. The Arab states, Asia, India, Iran, Central and South America also weighed in. Naturally, each major language layer brought subtle shifts in grammar and usage too. Hey—no pain, no gain. You want a rich language, you gotta deal with some issues over spelling consistency.

Happily for us, English never rejects a word because of its race, creed, or national origin. Let me prove it to you. Take this simple quiz to match each of the following words with its native language. Write the letter of the correct choice in the blank by the number.

Word	*Country of Origin*
1. decorum	a. Arabic
2. blarney	b. Russian
3. raconteur	c. Senegalese
4. carafe	d. Malayan
5. typhoon	e. Latin
6. yam	f. French
7. tsar	g. Celtic
8. ketchup	h. Yiddish
9. knish	i. French
10. aspic	j. Chinese

Answers: 1. e; 2. g; 3. i; 4. a; 5. j; 6. c; 7. b; 8. d; 9. h; 10. f.

You're Not Nuts

Now you understand why it's not your fault: English spelling *is* as screwy as you've always suspected. And now you know the reason: there aren't any spelling police rapping new-comers on the knuckles and admonishing, "Don't even be thinking of changing the language! No new words for you!" Just the opposite is true—English welcomes change and adapts accordingly.

But just because English spelling can seem as stable as Jell-O doesn't let you off the hook. As you read in chapter 1, if you can't spell a word correctly, you can't communicate clearly and correctly.

Don't Say We Didn't Try

A number of brave souls have attempted to regularize English spelling. They all failed, of course, but we give them high marks for effort.

Esperanto

The most famous attempt occurred around 1875, when Dr. Ludovic Zamenhof, an eye doctor, decided to invent a totally new language that actually made sense. His language, which he called Esperanto, has five vowels and twenty-three consonants. The spelling is easy and logical. Of course, no country has made Esperanto its national language. Some sources claim between one hundred thousand and two million people speak it, but when's the last time you heard people chatting away in Esperanto? Anyone?

International English Spelling Day

There's even an International English Spelling Day, held on October 9. On that day, the self-proclaimed Spelling Police exhort us to find misspellings—on signs, in newspapers, in books, on documents, and so on. Puh-leeze.

Koreans are big on spelling, even celebrating a National Spelling Day. In part, the day commemorates King Sejong the Great, the Fourth Monarch of the Yi Dynasty (c. 1440), who had his scholars develop a simple method of transcribing spoken Korean. The so-called Hangul alphabet resulted.

The Dictionary

"If you can't spell a word, just look it up!" your mother/father/teacher said in an exasperated tone. So why didn't early folks just consult the dictionary? Dictionaries are actually relatively recent inventions. They weren't around in Shakespeare's day (1564–1616), which is why the Bard spelled things the way he wanted, even his own name. Common variations include—but are far from limited to—*Shagsbere, Shaxpere, Shackerpere, Shaxpeare, Shakesspeare,* and *Shakespeare.* In 1869, George Wise published the *Autograph of William Shakespeare: Together with 4000 Ways of Spelling the Name According to English Orthography.*

Finally, someone invented an English dictionary. That someone was Robert Cawdrey in 1604, but it had only 3,000 words and skimpy definitions. About fifty years later, Thomas Blount published his *Glossographia*; Samuel Johnson came out with his famous dictionary in 1755.

Lexicography is the field of writing dictionaries.

One of America's first bestsellers wasn't a romance novel, a cookbook, or even a sex manual. No, it was the country's first spelling book, Noah Webster's *The American Spelling Book*. By 1816, more than five million copies had been sold. Sixteen years later, the number had soared past fifteen million. By the beginning of the Civil War, forty-two million copies were in the hands of Americans eager to improve their spelling. From 1876 to 1890, more than eleven million copies flew off the shelves. These numbers are even more impressive since at the time fewer than one hundred thousand people lived in Illinois and the entire population of New York was less than one third the present population of Manhattan.

Today *The Oxford English Dictionary* is the most complete English dictionary. The editors started this massive undertaking in 1860. It took them sixty-eight years to finish, so you can tell that we're talking about one big dictionary. Of course, it's multiple volumes—like an encyclopedia.

The word *dictionary* comes from the Latin word *dictio*, which means "word."

Cut to the Chase

English spelling is irregular, irritating, and downright infuriating because of the way the language developed. ▪

Chapter 3

Why People Misspell Words

■ ■ ■

"Why *do* people misspell words? Duh—because they don't know how to spell them," you mutter. Ah, but it's not quite so simple. When it comes to our children misspelling words, it's usually not their fault because they were taught idiotic methods of spelling, the worst being *invented spelling.* But everyone gets hammered by *sensational spelling,* deliberately misspelled trademarked words used in product placement. There are other reasons as well.

Many people misspell words because they write them so fast that they forget a letter or two. Often, they don't have the time to proofread. Then there are times that people do indeed spell the word correctly—but it's the wrong word in context. Other times, people mispronounce the words and thus misspell them. In this chapter, find out why you spell words incorrectly—so you can learn some easy ways to spell them correctly.

Invented Spelling: A Storee for U

Little Taylor Smyth-Framingham-Schwartz writes her first-grade story as follows: "HGnsk psky skuyq cl. SPhjk Wnnys plu IIkl."

"Read your story to me," said her teacher.

The tyke "reads" her story as follows: "Once upon a time, a beautiful princess who happened to be an oral surgeon met a terrible monster, but the monster wasn't so terrible after all—he was just in pain from an impacted wisdom tooth. After Dr. Beautiful Princess extracted the monster's tooth, he felt fine and dandy. He went to dental school, graduated at the top of his class, and joined the princess's dental practice. They lived happily every after."

"Excellent story, little Taylor Smyth-Framingham-Schwartz. You spelled the words beautifully," said the teacher.

I'm not making this up. Well, I am, but this story is based on truth: Little Taylor is being taught "invented spelling," a process whereby children invent spellings for words by arranging letters as they like. Children use their best judgments about spelling, "using whatever knowledge of sounds or visual patterns the writer has" (Bank Street College, 1997). Invented spelling is similar to new theories about potty training: apparently this is such a difficult skill that we wait until children are "ready." So what if a generation ago children were fully ready and potty trained by age two and now they're closer to age five? Who are we to tamper with nature?

Tamper away. In the past, spelling was usually taught as a separate subject, through memorization. As a result, people learned to spell. Fortunately, some elementary schools still use spelling books and treat spelling as a subject separate from the other language arts. However, far too many schools let children create their own language. How can you blame people for not being able to spell if they were never taught?

Sensational Spelling

Sensational spelling is intentionally misspelling a word to create a special effect, most often in advertising. Here are some examples:

Sensational Spelling	*Correct Spelling*
Crème	cream
Froot Loops	Fruit loops
Magick	magic
Krispy	crispy

Sensational spelling isn't as egregious as invented spelling, but it's evil in its own way because it plays with our heads. As someone who has been grading poor spelling for far too long, I'm familiar with the English teacher's version of the Stockholm syndrome: look at a misspelled word long enough and it starts to look correct. It isn't correct, but try telling that to your brain after a decade of reading it misspelled. Sensational spelling is especially common with brand names, so buyer beware.

Winnie the Pooh

Another reason that people misspell words is that they misread them. Try it yourself. Read the following anecdote about Winston Churchill. Then circle the eight misspelled words and complete the list that follows.

In 1946, Winston Churchill travelled to Fulton, Missouri, to deliver a speech and recieve a bust dedicated in his honor. A gorgoeus women approached the wartime Prime Minister of Britian in the isle. She said, "Mr. Churchill, I have few heros, but you are one of them. I have come over a hundred miles this morning for the unvieling of your bust." Churchill, who was known far and wide for his quick wit, replied, "Madam, I assure you in that regard I would gladly return the favor."

Misspelled Word	*Corrected Word*
_____	_____
_____	_____
_____	_____
_____	_____
_____	_____
_____	_____
_____	_____

Answers

Misspelled Word	*Corrected Word*
recieve	receive
gorgoeus	gorgeous
women	woman
Britian	Britain
isle	aisle
heros	heroes
unvieling	unveiling

Every time you write, run your spell-check and proofread. It's no guarantee that every word will be correctly spelled, but it will help you catch more spelling errors than not.

Homographs and Homophones

Words are often misspelled because they're the wrong words for the context, as you learned in this chapter. They're spelled just fine and dandy . . . but they're still the wrong words. That's because English has many words that are often confused. A lot. The most common culprits are *homographs* and *homophones*.

- *Homographs* are words with the same spelling and pronunciation but different meanings. For example: *bear* (animal) and *bear* (to endure).
- *Homophones* are words with the same pronunciation but different spellings and meanings. For example: *their, they're, there*.

Which Witch Is Which?

Try it yourself. Circle the correct word in each set of parentheses.

1. What did the grape say when it was stepped on? Nothing—but it let out a little (whine, wine).

2. A baker stopped making donuts after he got tired of the (hole, whole) thing.

3. A cardboard belt would be a (waist, waste) of paper.

4. It was an emotional wedding; even the cake was in (tiers, tears).

5. They tried to save him with an IV but it was all in (vein, vain).

6. Bakers trade bread recipes on a (knead, need)-to-know basis.

7. A hawk sat atop a church waiting to grab the sparrow because the hawk was a bird of (pray, prey).

8. Seven days without a pun makes one (weak, week).

9. The flock of politically ambitious doves decided to stage a (coupe, coup).

Kids were asked to write about the sea:

10. This is a picture of an octopus. It has eight (testicles, tentacles).

11. If you are surrounded by (see, sea), you are an island. If not, you are (incontinent, a continent).

12. I am not going to write about the sea. My baby brother is always screaming, my Dad keeps shouting at my Mom, and my big sister has just got pregnant, so I can't think about what to (right, write).

Answers: The second word in each pair is correct.

The following chart shows some of the most commonly confused words and their definitions.

Word Pair	Meaning
air/err/heir	atmosphere/to make a mistake/inheritor
all together/altogether	all at one time/completely
allowed/aloud	given permission/verbally
are/our	plural of *is*/belonging to us
ascent/assent	to move up/to agree
bare/bear	plain, undressed/animal, carry
base/bass	bottom part of an object, morally low, plate in baseball/musical instrument, male voice, type of fish
beau/bow	sweetheart/forward end of a ship, to bend from the waist, a device used to propel arrows, loops of ribbon
beat/beet	to defeat/vegetable
berth/birth	sleeping area on a ship/being born
boar/bore	male pig/tiresome person
bridal/bridle	pertaining to the bride/part of a horse's harness

Word Pair	Meaning
cell/sell	a small room/to trade
cent/scent	penny/aroma
cheap/cheep	not costly/bird sound
conscience/conscious	moral sense/awake
coup (koop)/coop	overturn, upset/cage or small enclosure
coup (koo)	act of overthrowing a government
also: coupe (kūp)	car
dam/damn	barrier/curse
dear/deer	beloved/animal
desert/dessert	arid region/sweet at the end of a meal
died/dyed	passed away/changed color
fair/fare	evenhanded, market, light coloring/food or drink, cost of transportation
flew/flue	past tense of "to fly"/fireplace exhaust pipe
foreword/forward	preface/onward
gorilla/guerrilla	ape/soldier
glutinous/gluttonous	sticky/eating voraciously
hangar/hanger	an airplane garage/a wire implement for hanging clothing in a closet
it's/its	contraction for *it is*/possessive form of *it*
leach/leech	dissolve/bloodsucking worm
lead/led	metal, to conduct/past tense of "to lead"
main/mane	primary/hair

Word Pair	*Meaning*
meat/meet	animal flesh/encounter
peace/piece	not war/segment
plane/plain	airship/not beautiful, obvious
pore/pour	skin opening, to study carefully/dispense from a container
principal/principle	main, head of a school/rule, standard, law, or assumption
read/reed	interpret written words/marsh grass
sea/see	ocean/vision
shear/sheer	cut/total
son/sun	male child/center of our solar system
stationary/stationery	fixed/writing paper
than/then	comparison/at that time
their/they're/there	possessive pronoun/contraction for *they are*/place
to/too/two	preposition/also/number
vain/vane/vein	egotistical/a device that shows wind direction/narrow water channel, blood vessel
way/weigh	method/consider, measure
wet/whet	make wet/sharpen
which/witch	that one/female wizard
who's/whose	contraction of *who is*/belonging to someone
wood/would	lumber/inclination
your/you're	possessive pronoun/contraction for *you are*

You Deserve a Break Today

How's about a bit more practice? Circle the correct word in each set of parentheses in these jokes.

Joke #1

(To, Too, Two) women (our, are) arguing about (witch, which) dog is smarter. (Their, They're) both very (vane, vein, vain) about their dogs.

SYLVIA: My dog is so smart, every morning he waits (four, for) the paper boy to come. Then he picks up the newspaper and brings it to me. (Its/It's) a pleasure.

MYRTLE: Yeah, I (no, know).

SYLVIA: How?

MYRTLE: *My* dog told me.

Joke #2

It was the day of the big sale. Big ads were the (mane, main) reason for the long line that formed by 8:30 A.M. all the (weigh, way) around the block. A small man tried to push to the front of the line, but no one (aloud, allowed) him to move (foreword, forward).

On the man's second attempt, he was knocked around a bit and (throne, thrown) to the end of the line again. As he got up the second time, he said, "That does it! If they hit me (won, one) more time, I don't open the (dam, damn) store!"

Answers: The last word in each pair is correct.

Voice the *s* between two vowels *(amuse, design, prison)* except after *a (base, parasite).* Exceptions include *disagree, opposite, analysis.*

Words Are Mispronounced

Many words are misspelled because they're mispronounced. For instance, Oprah Winfrey's name is misspelled: It was originally *Orpah,* a biblical character, but relatives mispronounced it. The misspelling stuck. Sadly, we can't mispronounce words and have our spellings stick. Happily, pronouncing a word correctly can help you spell it correctly.

English has many bizarre pronunciations. For instance, take *gh.*

- Before a vowel, *gh* becomes *g,* as in *ghost.*
- *Gh* can keep the *g* from softening, as in *ghetto.*
- *Gh* can be dropped, as in *freight.*
- At the end of a word it can be *f,* as in *cough.*

It does so much more too.

With words that start with *gn, kn, mn, pt, ps,* and *tm,* pronounce only the second letter.

Here are some of the most often mispronounced and misspelled words in English:

Correct Spelling	*Common Misspelling*
across	acrossed
affidavit	affidavid
Alzheimer's disease	old-timer's disease
Antarctic	Antartic
arctic	artic
athlete	athelete
clothes	cloths, close
duct tape	duck tape
escape	excape
especially	expecially
espresso	expresso
et cetera	excetera
fiscal	fisical
foliage	foilage
height	heighth
interpret	interpretate
jewelry	jewlery
larynx	larins
library	libary
mayonnaise	mannaise
miniature	miniture
nuclear	nucular
nuptial	nuptual
ordnance	ordinance
ostensibly	ostensively
parliament	parlament
perspire	prespire
prerogative	perogative

Correct Spelling	*Common Misspelling*
prescription	perscription
pronunciation	pronounciation
regardless	irregardless
relevant	revelant
sherbet	sherbert
supposedly	supposably

Cut to the Chase

People don't misspell words because they're stupid. People *do* misspell words because they're the victims of educational fraud, because advertisers play with our heads, and because people often write so fast that they leave out letters. English also has many words that are easily confused. Mispronouncing words makes it difficult to spell them correctly too. ▪

Chapter 4

How to Learn to Spell

■ ■ ■

Here's Mark Twain's plan for improving English spelling:

In Year 1, the useless letter "c" would be dropped to be replased either by "k" or "s," and likewise "x" would no longer be part of the alphabet. The only kase in which "c" would be retained would be the "ch" formation, which will be dealt with later. Year 2 might reform "w" spelling, so that "which" and "one" would take the same konsonant, wile in Year 3 might well abolish "y" replasing it with "i" and Iear 4 might fiks the "g/j" anomali wonse and for all.

Jenerally, then, the improvement would kontinue iear bai iear with Iear 5 doing awai with useless double konsonants, and Iears 6–12 or so modifaiing vowlz and the rimeining voist and unvoist konsonants. Bai Iear 15 or sou, it wud fainali bi posibl tu meik ius ov thi ridandant letez "c," "y," and "x"—bai now jast a memori in the maindz ov ould doderez—tu riplais "ch," "sh," and "th" rispektivli.

Fainali, xen, aafte sam 20 iers ov orxogrefkl riform, wi wud hev a lojikl, kohirnt speling in ius xrewawt xe Ingliy-spiking werld.

Mark Twain was the penname of Samuel Langhorne Clemens (1835–1910), American humorist, novelist, and lecturer. His most famous novels include *The Adventures of Huckleberry Finn* and *The Adventures of Tom Sawyer.* He was a good speller.

Soup's On

As you can tell, there's no doubt that it's easier to learn to spell than to read Twain's spelling "reforms," so let's start with a quick spelling pick-me-up. Read the following joke. Then circle the ten misspelled words, and complete the list that follows.

A concerned husband goes to the doctor to talk about his wife. He says, "I think my wife is deaf because she never hears me the first time and allways asks me to repete things."

"Well," the doctor replies, "go home tonight, stand about fifteen feet from her, and say something. If she doesn't reply, move five feet closer and say it again. Keep doing this untill we get an idea about the severity of her deafness."

The husband goes home and does exactly as the doctor instructed. He starts off fifteen feet from his wife in the kitchen as she is chopping some carrotts. He says in a corteous way, "Honey, what's for dinner? Is it something delicous?"

He hears no response, so he moves five feet closer.

This time he walks into her imaculate kitchen and says, "Are we having my favorite friccassee of chicken?" No reply. He moves five feet closer. Still no reply.

He finally gets really fed up, moves an inch away from her, and asks again, "Honey, what's for dinner?"

She replies, "For the forth time, we're having vegeteble stew."

Misspelled Word	Corrected Word
_____	_____
_____	_____
_____	_____
_____	_____
_____	_____
_____	_____
_____	_____
_____	_____
_____	_____

Answers

allways	always
repete	repeat
untill	until
carrotts	carrots
corteous	courteous

(Answers continued)

Misspelled Word	**Corrected Word**
delicous	delicious
imaculate	immaculate
friccassee	fricassee
forth	fourth
vegeteble	vegetable

A Method to This Madness

Here's my favorite technique for learning to spell unfamiliar or difficult words. It's fun, easy, and best of all, tried-and-true. It worked for me, and I was a hard case. Read the five steps and then use them on the ten words that follow.

 1. Read the word. Pronounce it aloud.

 2. Close your eyes and visualize the word. Spell it to yourself.

3. Check that you spelled the word correctly.

 4. Write the word.

 5. Look back at the word to check that you spelled it correctly.

Use the method to learn to spell these words:

1. across	6. receive
2. commercial	7. referred
3. exercise	8. relevant
4. maintenance	9. similar
5. opportunities	10. useful

Many people think they can predict how an English word is spelled from the way it's pronounced. Sometimes it works. Sometimes it doesn't.

How's It Going?

See how well you learned to spell these ten tough but useful words. Circle the correctly spelled word in each line.

1. referred	refferred	refered
2. exercise	excercise	ecersize
3. receive	recieve	receeve
4. opportunities	oportunities	opportunaties
5. useful	usefull	usefful
6. commercial	commercail	commercal
7. similar	simalar	simlar
8. maintenance	maintenence	maintinance
9. across	accross	acros
10. relevant	relevent	relavent

Answers: The first word in each row is correct.

Here are some additional techniques for learning how to spell new words. They're all relatively painless and quite simple. Best of all, they work great.

Look for Patterns

One of the most effective ways to learn to spell many words is to group them by similarities. You can use any patterns you like—word length, part of speech, initial letter, and so on—but I've found that the most useful groupings are based on spelling patterns. For instance, all the following words follow the vowel-consonant-consonant-vowel pattern, which we'll call VCCV for short.

VCCV Pattern

absent	disgust	impel	pummel
abstract	dismal	imprint	signet
address	dispel	indulgent	spectrum
bombastic	distinct	inkling	syntax
compel	excess	insect	tendril
confession	expected	instinct	tranquil
cosmic	falcon	limpid	transcendent
damsel	fantastic	mandrill	wistful

As you practice learning how to spell these words, divide them at the consonants, like this: *confes/sion, cos/mic,* and *sig/net.*

The following pattern is VCV—one consonant between two vowels. Recognizing this pattern can help you learn to spell these tricky words more easily.

VCV Pattern

amputate	crusade	humane	prelate
bogus	cupid	hypnotize	primate
butane	deny	improvise	profile
cement	elope	incubate	rayon
crocus	foment	nomad	recited

Everyone Loves a Puzzle

Another great way to learn to spell is to enjoy word games such as acrostics, crossword puzzles, and so on. They're easy to carry and complete when you have a few spare moments. For instance, ever wait in the dentist's office? Take the ten minutes (or two hours) to do a crossword puzzle and polish your spelling skills. Ditto for standing in line at the Department of Motor Vehicles, the airport, and the post office or waiting while you're in labor. Some of those kids take a long time to push out.

Try it now. Complete the following crossword puzzle to practice the words you just learned with the VCCV and VCV patterns. This puzzle uses twelve words. Choose from the following twenty-five:

confession	insect	disgust	impel
crocus	cupid	absent	wistful
primate	deny	tranquil	indulgent
inkling	cement	syntax	tendril
prelate	amputate	rayon	elope
butane	distinct	falcon	bogus
bombastic			

(puzzle on following page)

ACROSS
3 bird
6 concrete
7 member of the ape family
10 calm
11 fake

DOWN
1 bug
2 missing
4 cut off
5 force
6 flower
8 hint
9 fabric type

Answers

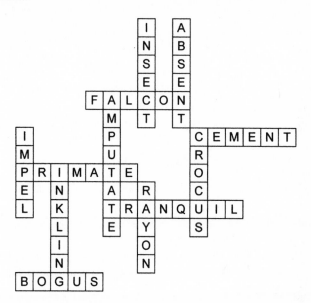

Divide and Conquer

Divide big words into groups of up to three letters to learn them part by part. This can help you remember many larger words or those with tricky letter sequences. Here are some examples for you to try now:

acknowledge	admirably	admonition	alter
animosity	assignment	barbarities	colonel
concomitant	consequential	constructive	correction
courtesy	detour	devoid	espionage
exacting	expressionless	faltering	forbidding

generosity	grimace	handiwork	hostility
incidentally	indignity	inevitably	intimidated
inventory	involuntary	jabber	manifestation
minutely	neutralize	nominal	nonentity
piety	porcine	powerlessness	punctilious
reinforce	revulsion	rigorous	scandalous
spectacular	speculative	subtle	succumb
superbly	unobtrusive	unprintable	unresponsive

At the Zoo

Read the following joke. Then choose the correct spelling of each word in parentheses.

One day, a mime visits the zoo and attempts to earn some money as a street performer. As soon as he starts to draw a crowd, the zookeeper grabs him and drags him into his office.

The zookeeper says, "A gorilla, the zoo's most popular attraction, died suddenly, and we're afraid that attendance at the zoo will fall off. Would you dress up as the gorilla until we can get another gorilla? We really need you to take this (assinment, assignment)." So desperate that he's willing to accept the (indignaty, indignity), the mime accepts the offer.

So the next morning, before the crowd arrives, the mime puts on the gorilla suit and enters the cage. He performs (admirebly, admirably) and does a (spectaculer, spectacular) job. Best of all, the mime loves the work. He can sleep all he wants, play whenever he chooses, and make fun of people, and he draws larger crowds than he ever did as a mime on the street. However, eventually the crowd tires of him, and he tires of just swinging on auto tires. He notices that the people are paying more attention to the lion in the next cage. Not wanting to lose the audience's attention, the mime climbs to the top of his cage, crawls across a partition, and dangles from the top of the lion's cage.

Of course, this makes the lion furious and he (grimases, grimaces) with (hostilaty, hostility), but the crowd loves it. At the end of the day, the zookeeper comes and gives the mime a raise for being such a good attraction.

Well, this goes on for some time; the mime keeps taunting the lion, the crowd grows larger, and the mime's salary keeps going up. (Inevitibly, Inevitably), a problem arises.

One day when the mime is dangling over the top of the lion's cage, he slips and falls. The mime is terrified. The lion raises himself up and prepares to pounce. The mime is so scared that he begins to run around the cage with the lion in hot pursuit.

Finally, the mime is so (intimadated, intimidated) that he starts screaming, "Help! Help me!" The lion is quick and pounces. The mime soon finds himself flat on his back looking up at the angry lion. The lion says, "Shut up, you idiot, or we'll both lose our jobs."

Answers: The second word in each pair is correct.

Use Memory Tricks

Memory tricks—*mnemonics*—can help you remember how to spell words. For example, there's an *e* in *envelope* and an *e* in *stationery* (writing paper). Come up with your own memory tricks—but don't make them more difficult than the words you're trying to remember how to spell!

Learn Spelling Rules

Believe it or not, English spelling *does* follow some rules. Here's a famous little ditty:

I before *e*
Except after *c*
Or when sounded as *a*
As in *neighbor* and *weigh*
It's the *other* way. (that is *e* before *i)*

Here are some examples:

i *before* e	*except after* c	*or when sounded as* a
mischief	receive	eight
believe	conceited	weight
field	ceiling	freight
achieve	perceive	beige

Naturally, there are some exceptions:

friend	either	foreign	seize
neither	leisure	weird	Fahrenheit

codeine   glacier   financier   height
counterfeit   protein   forfeit

You're On

Figure out which words are misspelled. Then fix 'em.

1. greif   6. foreign
2. percieve   7. surviellance
3. reign   8. efficeint
4. protien   9. shreik
5. releif   10. receeve

Answers: 1. grief; 2. perceive; 3. correct; 4. protein; 5. relief;
6. correct; 7. surveillance; 8. efficient; 9. shriek; 10. receive.
Not to worry: I cover more spelling rules later in this book,
especially in chapters 9, 10, and 11.

Orthography is the way that we write words.
Phonology is the way we say them.

Cut to the Chase

You *can* learn to spell. Start with my five-step method. Then
look for patterns in words, do word puzzles, divide words
into smaller parts, create memory tricks to help you remember important but tricky words, and learn spelling rules. ▪

Chapter 5

Vowel Movement 1:
Phun with Phonics

■ ■ ■

Did you hear the one about— You heard that one? Okay, so I'll bet that you haven't heard *this* one. As you're reading it, circle the ten misspelled words, and complete the list that follows.

An Illinois man left the fridig streets of Chicago for a vacaton in Florida. His wife was on a bussiness trip and was planning to meet him there the next day. The occassion? Their anniversary. When he reached his hotel, he decided to send his wife a quick e-mail.

Looking all accross the desk, he was unable to find the scrap of paper on which he had written her e-mail address, so he did his best to type it in from memory. Unfortunatly, he missed one letter, and his note was directed instead to an elderly preacher's wife whose husband had died the day before. When the greiving widow checked her e-mail, she took one look at the monator, let out a peircing scream, and fell to the floor dead.

At the sound, her family rushed into the room and saw the following note on the screen:

Dearest Wife,

Just got checked in. Everything prepared for your arrival tommorrow.

Your loving husband.

P.S. Sure is hot down here.

Misspelled Word	*Corrected Word*
_____	_____
_____	_____
_____	_____
_____	_____
_____	_____
_____	_____
_____	_____
_____	_____
_____	_____

Answers

fridig	frigid
vacaton	vacation
bussiness	business
occassion	occasion
accross	across
unfortunatly	unfortunately
greiving	grieving

(Answers continued)

Misspelled Word

monator

peircing

tommorrow

Corrected Word

monitor

piercing

tomorrow

Phonics is the connection between sounds or groups of sounds and letters. It's the basis for reading a language.

What Are Phonics?

We decided that approaching spelling from the way English works makes a lot of sense. After all, understanding the basics of the language can help you figure out how to spell many, many important and useful words.

The most basic kind of knowledge required for good English spelling involves *phonics* knowledge, the knowledge of common letter-sound relationships. For instance, you know that the sound /k/ can be represented by *c, k,* or *ck* spellings. In this chapter and several subsequent ones, we'll have some vowel movements, thanks to phonics. (This book is too short to cover all the phonics patterns in English, so we'll just cover some key ones that will help you become a better speller.)

Overview: Sound and Sense

Each English vowel has two sounds: one short and one long.

Short Vowel Sounds

The short vowels are the five single letter vowels, *a, e, i, o,* and *u* when they produce the sounds /a/ as in *at*, /e/ as in *elm*, /i/ as in *sit*, /o/ as in *hop*, and /u/ as in *cup*. We put a short curved line over a vowel to indicate it has a short sound, like this: ă.

You only need one letter to spell a short vowel sound.

as   bed   ill   cot   up

The term "short vowel" doesn't mean that you say them fast. No, I don't have any idea why they're called short, and please don't send me e-mails with your theories. I'd far prefer chocolate and roses.

Long Vowel Sounds

The long vowel sound is the same as the name of each vowel: *a, e, i, o,* and *u*. You can hear the long sounds in *ape, eat, eye, hoe,* and *you*. We put a long line over a vowel to indicate that it has a long sound like this: ā.

You have to add a second vowel to spell a long sound. There are two ways to do this:

- The second vowel is next to the first one in the VVC pattern: *coat, paid, due.*
- The second vowel is separated from the first vowel by a consonant in the VCV pattern: *made, tide, hide.*

If the second vowel is separated from the first by *two* or more spaces, it doesn't affect the first one. This is the VCCV pattern in which the first vowel remains short. Thus, doubling a consonant keeps another vowel from getting close enough to the first one to change its sound from short to long. Here are some examples:

short a	long a	long a		short i	long i	long i
madder	maid	made		dinner	dine	diner
VCCV				**VCCV**		

The Schwa

Every vowel has a third sound—the *schwa*—in an unstressed syllable. The schwa is the most frequent vowel sound in English. It's shown by the linguistic symbol ə. For instance, the /ə/ is the sound made by the *o* in *lesson.*

Here's an easy saying to help you remember the way that vowels work in English: A cat says "meow."

Making Phonics Work for You!

I've already reminded you that English is about as consistent as the weather in April. Nonetheless, there are some phonics rules that can make it easier for you to figure out how to spell many critical words. Here are four:

1. When a single vowel occurs in the middle of a word (or syllable), it usually has the short sound, as in the

following examples: *bat, hit, set, mitt, got, nut, lap, red, shot,* and *hut.* This rule can help you figure out how to spell some words in confusing word pairs, such as *rack* vs. *rake, lack* vs. *lake, tack* vs. *take, smock* vs. *smoke,* and so on.

2. When a word ends with a single vowel (or syllable), it usually has a long sound. For example: *go, he, ago, hyperbole.*

3. When two vowels are next to each other in the same word (or syllable), the first vowel usually has a long sound and the second vowel stays silent. For example: *rain, goal.* This rule is traditionally taught with this clever ditty: "When two vowels go walking, the first does the talking." Despite the cleverness of the ditty, this rule has many exceptions, such as *oi* ("moist" and "boil") and the *oo* spelling of /u/.

4. Vowels are usually short before two consonants (VCC), as in *rotten, butler, tack, tick, back, buck, bank, bark, bulk, hack, hock, hark, task, wilt, milk, malt, add, with, path, sash,* and *wish.* Extending this further, if you hear a word with a short vowel sound followed by a *k* sound, there is a good chance that the *k* sound will be spelled by *ck* to give you the two consonants. In other cases, you should be able to hear the two final consonants: *-sh, -lk, -rk, -sk, -th, -ch,* and *-nd.*

Naturally, since this is English, there are a lot of weird patterns that don't follow any rules. You just have to suck it up and memorize them. For instance:

- *igh* as in "high" and "sight."
- *ost* as in "most" uses the long sound but "lost" and "cost" don't.
- *ow* has two different sounds as in "low" and "cow."
- *ed* has three different sounds as in "lifted," "dropped," and "moneyed."
- *oo* has two different sounds as in "book" and "loose."
- *-sion, -tion,* and *-cian* are pronounced as "shun."
- *ed* has three different sounds as in "lifted," "walked," and "played."
- *oo* has two different sounds as in "book" and "loose."
- *-sion, -tion,* and *-cian* are pronounced as "shun."
- *ough* has at least seven different sounds, including "bough," "cough," "tough," "thought," and "through."

Party Time

Underline the incorrectly spelled word in each pair and correct it. Use the phonics guidelines that you just learned.

1. aborigine	awt	_____
2. asterik	through	_____
3. catastroph	sesame	_____
4. whisc	alibi	_____
5. anemone	hindsite	_____
6. obelick	raffle	_____
7. shanghai	adobee	_____
8. gibberiss	alkali	_____
9. knich	baffle	_____
10. calliope	squich	_____

11. al fresco	tuff	_____
12. sawt	buffalo	_____
13. archipelagoe	impresario	_____
14. couff	children	_____
15. patricain	loose	_____

Answers: (1) ought; (2) asterisk; (3) catastrophe; (4) whisk; (5) hindsight; (6) obelisk; (7) abobe; (8) gibberish; (9) knish; (10) squish; (11) tough; (12) sought; (13) archipelago; (14) cough; (15) patrician.

There are so many words that don't follow these rules that we even have a name for them: "sight words." They include *the, were, who, you,* and *are*—and many more. These are small words, but mighty ones, well worth spelling correctly. Many people confuse *where, wear,* and *were,* for instance. Not you!

Now, let's look a little more closely at /a/. Such a sweet little letter, and it does come first in the alphabet.

Patterns for Spelling /a/

The Long /a/ Sound

The long /a/ can be spelled the following ways:

a-e	*ai*	*ay*
cellophane	rainbow	yesterday
counterpane	available	gray
celibate	praise	away

Long /a/ This a Way

Complete the following crossword puzzle to practice spelling words with the long /ā/ spelled /ai/. This puzzle uses eight words. Choose from the following twelve words.

ascertain	brain	chain	drain
grain	legerdemain	moraine	plantain
porcelain	ptomaine	quatrain	terrain

ACROSS
4 food poisoning
5 china
7 to figure out
8 banana-like vegetable

DOWN
1 poetic term
2 a ridge, mound, or irregular mass of unstratified glacial drift, chiefly boulders, gravel, sand, and clay.
3 trickery, deception, sleight-of-hand
6 land

Answers

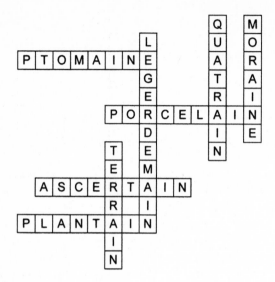

/A/ Sort

Sort these words according to their spelling pattern for the long /a/. Write each word in the correct column.

Wednesday	abstain	gait
throughway	castaway	laser
desolate	straight	displacement
disgraceful	disarray	urbane
entertainment	trailer	sashay

a-e	*ai*	*ay*
_____	_____	_____
_____	_____	_____
_____	_____	_____
_____	_____	_____
_____	_____	_____

Answers

displacement	entertainment	disarray
urbane	trailer	sashay
laser	straight	throughway
disgraceful	gait	castaway
desolate	abstain	Wednesday

Many words have entered English from French. The words that end in é have the long /ā/ sound. For example: *résumé, canapé, consommé, exposé, Salomé, café au lait,* **and** *pâpier-maché.*

The /ä/ sound is spelled *ar* as in *star.* The /ãr/ sound is spelled *are* as in *dare* and *air* as in *pair.*

Cut to the Chase

Learning the basics of phonics—the knowledge of common letter-sound relationships—can help you improve your spelling because it teaches you how English works. It also makes great club conversation. ▪

Chapter 6

Vowel Movement 2: Phonics Wirked 4 Me

■ ■ ■

Speaking of spelling, here's a news flash:

The European Commission has just announced an agreement whereby English rather than German will be the official language of the EU. As part of the negotiations, Her Majesty's Government conceded that English spelling had some room for improvement and has accepted a five-year phase-in plan that would be known as "Euro-English."

In the first year, "s" will replace the soft "c." Sertainly, this will make the sivil servants jump with joy. The hard "c" will be dropped in favor of the "k." This should klear up konfusion and keyboards kan have one less letter.

There will be growing publik enthusiasm in the sekond year, when the troublesome "ph" will be replased with the "f." This will make words like "fotograf" 20% shorter. In the 3rd year, publik akseptanse of the new spelling kan be expekted to reach the stage where more komplikated changes are possible.

Governments will enkourage the removal of double letters, which have always ben a deterent to akurate speling. Also, al wil agre that the horible mes of the silent "e's" in the language is disgraseful, and they should go away.

By the 4th yar, peopl wil be reseptiv to steps such as replasing "th" with "z" and the "w" with "v." During the fifz yar, ze unesesary "o" kan be dropd from vords kontaining "ou" and similar changes vud of kors be aplid to ozer kombinations of leters.

After zis fifz yar, ve vil hav a reli sensibl riten styl. Zer vil be no mor trubls or difikultis and evrivun vil find it easy tu understand ech ozer.

Ze drem vil finali kum tru!

Warm Up

Time to flex your spelling muscles. Read the following jokes. Then choose the correct spelling of each word in parentheses.

Joke #1

A (1. cite, site) (2. foreman, forman) who had ten very lazy men working for him figured out a new way to (3. decieve, deceive) them into doing some work for once.

"I've got a super-easy job today for the (4. lazest, laziest) one among you," he announced. "Will the most lazy man please put his hand up?"

Nine hands went up.

"Why didn't you put your hand up?" he asked the tenth man.

"(5. Two, Too, To) much trouble," came the reply.

Joke #2

> TEACHER: "If you already had one dollar and you
> asked your (6. father, farther) for another, how
> many dollars would you have then?"
>
> VINCENT: "A dollar."
>
> TEACHER (*sadly*): "You don't know your
> (7. arithametic, arithmetic)."
>
> VINCENT (*sadly*): "You don't know my father."

Joke #3

"Do you believe in life after death?" the boss asked the
newest of his (8. employees, employes).

"Yes, sir," the recent (9. recruit, recriut) replied.

"Well, then, everything is just fine in that case," the
boss continued. "After you left early to go to your grand-
mother's (10. funerel, funeral) yesterday, she stopped by
to see you."

Answers: 1. site; 2. foreman; 3. deceive; 4. laziest; 5. Too;
6. father; 7. arithmetic; 8. employees; 9. recruit; 10. funeral.

**"The English have no respect for their language, and
will not teach their children to speak it. They spell it
so abominably that no man can teach himself what it
sounds like. It is impossible for an Englishman to
open his mouth without making some other Englishman hate or despise him. German and Spanish are
accessible to foreigners: English is not accessible
even to Englishmen." — *George Bernard Shaw***

The Eyes Have It: Spelling Short /i/ and Long /i/

You discovered in chapter 5 that learning to identify sound-spelling patterns will help you spell many useful words correctly—all that phonics information. Let's apply it to the letter /i/.

As you might expect, given the vagaries of English, the letter /i/ can be spelled many different ways. For instance, short /i/ is spelled *i* as in *pig*, but long /i/ can be spelled *i-e* as in *time*, *i* as in *kind*, *y* as in *fly*, *igh* as in *night*, and *ie* as in *pie*. Below are the patterns you can find with the short /i/ and long /i/ sounds and some examples of useful spelling words with these patterns.

Some Words with Short /i/

innings	quit
things	biscuit
rivers	plastic

Some Words with Long /i/

i-e	*I*	*y*
quiet	lightning	preoccupy
quite	idle	pacify

igh	*ie*	
blight	tie	
fright	belie	

Eye Candy

Fill in the following chart by sorting the words by their sound and spelling for the short /i/ and long /i/. If there's nothing good on television, why not add as many other words with the same spelling patterns and sounds as you can? (Hey, it beats taking out the garbage.)

belie	bite	brilliant	copyright
crime	exemplify	fie	icicle
icing	identical	ideology	illegally
illegible	indemnify	instantaneous	intensify
island	lie	lime	might
mudpie	petrify	sight	slime
solidify	time	twilight	vie
weathertight	withered		

short /i/ long /i/

i	*i-e*	*i*
_____	_____	_____
_____	_____	_____
_____	_____	_____
_____	_____	_____
_____	_____	_____

short /i/ long /i/

y	igh	ie
_____	_____	_____
_____	_____	_____
_____	_____	_____
_____	_____	_____
_____	_____	_____

Answers

i	*i-e*	*i*
instantaneous	lime	ideology
illegally	slime	icing
illegible	crime	icicle
withered	bite	identical
brilliant	time	island

y	*igh*	*ie*
petrify	might	lie
solidify	weathertight	mudpie
exemplify	copyright	fie
indemnify	twilight	vie
intensify	sight	belie

007: License to Spell

James Bond made the *double o* famous, but long before he
was spying for Her Majesty's Secret Service, the *oo* was

making waves on the phonics front. As you read in chapter 5, *oo* is spelled only one way but said two different ways. It is pronounced as in *book* and as in *loose*.

Here are some examples:

oo as in book

cocoon
hood

oo as in loose

food
noon

OO La La

Fill in the chart below by sorting the words by their sound and spelling for double *oo*.

anteroom	bedroom	buffoon	choose
heirloom	livelihood	macaroon	neighborhood
taboo	vamoose	yahoo	zoo

oo as in book

_____

_____

_____

_____

_____

_____

oo as in loose

_____

_____

_____

_____

_____

_____

Answers

buffoon
heirloom

bedroom
yahoo

(Answers continued)

oo as in book	**oo as in loose**
livelihood	vamoose
neighborhood	choose
anteroom	zoo
macaroon	taboo

Try It in Ink

Complete the following crossword puzzle to practice spelling words with the short /i/, long /i/, and double oo. This puzzle uses ten words. Choose from the following twelve words:

bassoon	caboose	exemplify
goose	identical	ideology
illegible	papoose	petrify
quit	quite	withered

ACROSS

3 musical instrument
4 native American baby carrier
5 show or prove, illustrate by example
8 dried up
9 unable to be read
10 belief system

DOWN

1 last car on a train
2 turn to stone; terrify
6 the same
7 type of bird that makes a delicious holiday meal

Answers

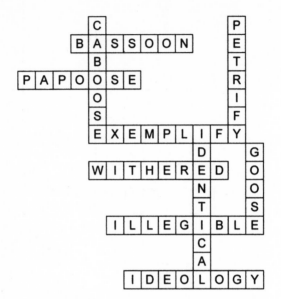

Blend It

As with *oo,* the letters *ea* can be pronounced in several different ways. Learning these sounds will help you spell these words correctly. Pretty swell, eh?

Often, *ea* sounds like the long /e/ as in *peace.* However, *ea* can also be pronounced as the short /e/ as in *spread* and the long /a/ as in *break.* It can also have the long /o/ sound as in *bureau* and the long /u/ sound as in *beauty.* Here are some more examples:

ea with the long /e/ sound	*ea with the short /e/ sound*	*ea with the long /a/ sound*
create	ready	great
please	instead	steak

ea with the long /o/ sound	*ea with the long /u/ sound*
plateau	beautiful
chateau	beautician

Fill in the chart below by sorting the words by their sound and spelling for *ea*.

bear	beau	beauteous	beautify
breaker	bureaucrat	chapeaux	Chesapeake
pear	pleasure	ready	squeak
tease	thread		

ea with the long /e/ sound	*ea with the short /e/ sound*	*ea with the long /a/ sound*
_____	_____	_____
_____	_____	_____
_____	_____	_____

ea with the long /o/ sound	*ea with the long /u/ sound*
_____	_____
_____	_____
_____	_____

Answers

ea with the long /e/ sound	**ea with the short /e/ sound**	**ea with the long /a/ sound**
Chesapeake	ready	breaker
tease	pleasure	bear
squeak	thread	pear

ea with the long /o/ sound	**ea with the long /u/ sound**
beau	beautify
chapeaux	beauteous
bureaucrat	

Diphthongs

Diphthongs sound like they'd be beachwear, maybe cute flip-flops or panties. Nope—they're two vowel sounds pronounced as one sound. You read about them briefly earlier in chapter 2. Learning to identify diphthongs will help you spell many good words. We don't have time or world enough for all the diphthongs, so here's just a taste of their deliciousness.

- The diphthongs /ou/ and /ow/ sound like the vowels in *count* and *owl*.
- The diphthongs /oy/ and /oi/ sound like the vowels in *boy* and *coin*.

The following words are some examples. As you read each word, say it aloud. Listen to the vowel sound. Circle the diphthong that makes the sound.

/ou/	/ow/	/oy/	/oi/
found	scow	joy	boil
shout	down	enjoy	voice
our	downstage	toy	points

Fill in the chart that follows by sorting the words by the spelling of their diphthongs.

asteroid	brown	celluloid	corduroy
destroy	devour	disavow	dour
kowtow	mountain	tabloid	viceroy

/ou/	/ow/	/oy/	/oi/
____	____	____	____
____	____	____	____
____	____	____	____

Answers

/ou/	/ow/	/oy/	/oi/
dour	brown	corduroy	celluloid
devour	kowtow	destroy	asteroid
mountain	disavow	viceroy	tabloid

Revisiting an Old Friend: The Schwa

Remember our friend the schwa? It looks like an upside down e. It is written like this: ə. It's an unstressed vowel, the most common sound in English. The schwa can be spelled many ways, just like many other sounds. Here are some examples of words with the schwa:

schwa spelled a	*schwa spelled e*	*schwa spelled i*
a in about	e in taken	i in mechanical
a in sofa	e in happen	i in aluminum

schwa spelled o	*schwa spelled u*
o in eloquent	u in circus
o in color	u in futuristic

Fill in the chart below by sorting the words by the spelling of their schwa.

alike	given	hundred	imagine	observe
pencil	seconds	succeed	woman	Venus

schwa spelled a	*schwa spelled e*	*schwa spelled i*
_____	_____	_____
_____	_____	_____

schwa spelled o	*schwa spelled u*
_____	_____
_____	_____

Answers

schwa spelled a	*schwa spelled e*	*schwa spelled i*
alike	given	imagine
woman	hundred	pencil

(Answers continued)

schwa spelled o   **schwa spelled u**

observe   succeed

seconds   Venus

Cut to the Chase

Mastering the fundamentals of phonics is a great way to get a big bang for your spelling buck. That's because it helps you understand letter–sound correspondences. ▦

Chapter 7

Vowel Movement 3: Spelling Consonants

■ ■ ■

"I've just had the most awful time," said a man to his colleagues. "First I got angina pectoris, then arteriosclerosis. Just as I was recovering, I got psoriasis. They gave me several hypodermics of antibiotics, and to top it all, tonsillitis was followed by appendectomy."

"Wow! How did you pull through?" his colleagues asked in a sympathetic manner.

"I don't know," the man replied. "Toughest spelling test I ever had."

Hit the Ground Running

Keep those spelling muscles flexed! Underline the incorrectly spelled word in each line and correct it. Spoiler Warning: These are thorny words, but I know you're up to the challenge.

Word	*Word*	*Word*	*Corrected Word*
1. accidentally	catagory	accommodate	_____
2. independence	hygiene	enviroment	_____
3. foreign	ridiculous	hemorhage	_____
4. parallel	counterfeit	neice	_____
5. priviledge	schedule	seize	_____
6. maintenance	judgment	changable	_____
7. ommitted	caterpillar	harass	_____
8. temperamental	grammer	automatic	_____
9. acquainted	photographic	argueing	_____
10. cantaloupe	khaki	cemetary	_____
11. hieght	knowledgeable	kiosk	_____
12. embarrass	laryngitis	irritible	_____
13. unaimus	leisure	liable	_____
14. congratulate	library	masuline	_____
15. forty	techneek	mezzanine	_____

Answers

1. category
2. environment
3. hemorrhage
4. niece
5. privilege
6. changeable
7. omitted
8. grammar
9. arguing
10. cemetery
11. height
12. irritable
13. unanimous
14. masculine
15. technique

Now that you've learned many vowel sounds, let's do the same with some consonant sounds. Remember: the more sounds you master, the more bang you get for your spelling buck.

No English word ends with *v*. The ending is always *ve*, as in *love*, *receive*, and *sleeve*.

Spelling the Sound /k/

■ buccaneer or buckaneer?
■ racoon or raccoon?
■ mica or micca? Or maybe micka? How about mika?

k or c?
k or cc?
k or k?
k or ck?

It's all so confusing! But not to worry—you'll soon have the answer to this vexing question that's been keeping you up at night. The /k/ sound can be spelled in any one of four ways: *c, cc, k, ck*.

/k/ Spelled c

"C" is the most common spelling for "k," and you can find it anywhere in a word. Here are some examples:

/k/ spelled c at the beginning of a word	/k/ spelled c in the middle of a word	/k/ spelled c at the end of a word
compliment	actor	public
confident	bacon	arsenic

/k/ Spelled cc

The *c* is often doubled to keep the vowel short, as in these words: *stucco, Mecca, baccalaureate, tobacco, occupy.*

/k/ Spelled k or ck

K or *ck* can be used for the sound of *c.* How can you tell? These two patterns are often used before an *e, i,* or *y.*

/k/ Spelled k Before e	/k/ Spelled k Before i	/k/ Spelled k Before y
sketch	kinship	tricky
token	skinny	flaky
keratosis	dyskinesia	kyphosis

/k/ Spelled ck Before e	/k/ Spelled ck Before i	/k/ Spelled ck Before y
darkest	rocking	lucky
blackest	ducking	finicky
frolicked	picking	sticky

And while we're here, *ck* always follows a short vowel, as these examples show: *clock, wrecks,* and *sack.* The letter k follows any other sound, as shown in these examples: *cork, duke,* and *peek.*

Yak is an exception, but unless you've decided to become a yak farmer in a remote Himalayas village, you're in the clear ignoring this.

Try It in Ink

Complete the following crossword puzzle to practice spelling words with /k/. This puzzle uses ten words. Choose from the following twelve words:

chaos	conjugal	cactus
choleric	comprise	cocoa
turmeric	connoisseur	succulent
concierge	mackintosh	flaky

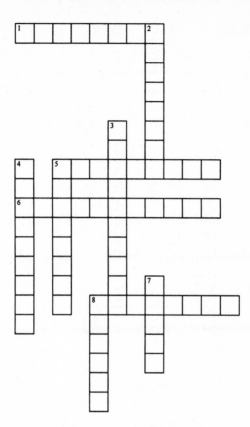

ACROSS

1 spice
5 person who has charge of the entrance to a building
6 expert
8 filled with rage

DOWN

2 made of
3 raincoat
4 moist, juicy
5 relating to marriage, especially the relations of a husband and wife
7 having small, thin pieces
8 desert plant

Answers

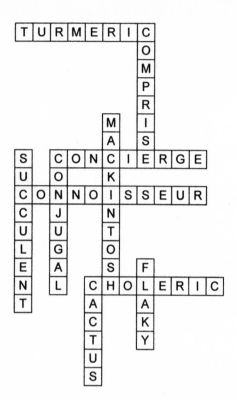

Spelling the Sound /j/

Why is it "Here comes the judge" rather than "Here comes the juje" or even "Here comes the juge"? Ah, it's another of the delightful vagaries of English, that tricky vixen. As with /k/, we're got some variations when it comes to the sound /j/: *j*, *g*, and *dge*. They can all carry the /j/ sound.

/j/ Spelled j

The letter *j* is usually used for the /j/ sound (notice: not always) if it is followed by an *a, o,* or *u.* Check out these examples:

/j/ Spelled j Before a	/j/ Spelled j Before o	/j/ Spelled j Before u
Benjamin	jogging	justified
Japan	majority	injured
adjacent	job	juvenile

/j/ Spelled g

The letter *g* is usually used to give the /j/ sound before an *e, i,* or *y,* as the following examples show.

/j/ Spelled g Before e	/j/ Spelled g Before i	/j/ Spelled g Before y
gentle	aging	Egyptologist
gem	ginger	gymnasium

/j/ Spelled dge

The letters *dge* are usually used if /j/ follows a short vowel sound, as the following examples show: *judge, budget, gadget,* and *partridge.*

The letters *j, v, k, w,* and *x* are never doubled.

You Deserve a Break

Yes, you do, and completing a quick puzzle is a lot less fattening than reaching for the chips and dip. Underline the incorrectly spelled word in each pair and correct it. Use the phonics guidelines that you just learned.

1.	galousie	jalousie	_____
2.	aging	ajing	_____
3.	algebra	aljebra	_____
4.	ginjer	ginger	_____
5.	adjacent	adjasent	_____
6.	jymnasium	gymnasium	_____
7.	jaguar	gaguar	_____
8.	smudge	smuge	_____
9.	buget	budget	_____
10.	majority	magority	_____

Answers: 1. jalousie; 2. aging; 3. algebra; 4. ginger; 5. adjacent; 6. gymnasium; 7. jaguar; 8. smudge; 9. budget; 10. majority.

Spelling the Sound /ch/

Are you getting a little *twitchy* with all this spelling stuff? Not to worry. Even though the sound /ch/ can be spelled two ways—*tch* and *ch*—the rule is simple: it's spelled *tch* after a short vowel and *ch* in any other instance. Here are some examples: *witch, satchel, botch, kitchen, hatchet,* and *escutcheon.*

I saved the best for last: the exceptions. Sadly, there are a handful, including *which, rich, much, such, touch, bachelor, attach, sandwich,* and *ostrich.*

The sound /kw/ is always spelled *qu*, so that's easy.
For instance: *quack, queasy, quibble, qualification,
quantity, quarry, quay, quartz,* and *quadrant.*

Shaken, Not Stirred

Sometimes it's tricky figuring out how to spell a word
because of its sound. Often, two or more letters seem to
blend together. You're not hearing wrong: they *are* blending
together. Not surprisingly, we call these *blends.* Clever, eh?
If you can hear all the letters in the blends, the odds are
good that you'll be able to spell the word correctly. Here
are some of the most common blends to watch for as you
encounter complex words.

Blend	Examples
bl	blanket, blunder
br	broken, Braille, brusque
ch	chafe, chaise lounge, chaos
cl	climate, clique
cr	cracker, credence, criteria
dr	dreadful, drinkable
fl	flood, florescent, flourish
fr	refrigerator, French
gl	globe, glamorous, glimpse
gr	group, Grecian
pl	platform, plankton, plateau
pr	protect, preempt,

Blend	Examples
sc	scratch, scorch, premier, prerequisite
scr	screech
sh	shred
sk	sketch
st	stripe, struggling
sw	swindle
th	throat
tr	transportation, tremendous, treasure
tw	twinkle

Find the Blend

Circle the blends in these words:

1. broach	6. claret	11. breath
2. grievous	7. drudgery	12. chasm
3. plausible	8. fluctuate	13. drought
4. playwright	9. cliché	14. glossary
5. criticize	10. cholesterol	15. breathe

Answers: 1. *br*oach; 2. *gr*ievous; 3. *pl*ausible; 4. *pl*aywright; 5. *cr*iticize; 6. *cl*aret; 7. *dr*udgery; 8. *fl*uctuate; 9. *cl*iché; 10. *cho*-lesterol; 11. *br*eath; 12. *ch*asm; 13. *dr*ought; 14. *gl*ossary; 15. *br*eathe.

Find the Word

Now, find these fifteen words in the word find puzzle. The words can be listed up, down, or on the diagonal. Each word contains an initial blend.

Britain	choose	clique	pledge
procession	Briton	crescendo	fluent
broccoli	grip	grotesque	grudge
gruesome	procrastinate	prominent	

(puzzle on following page)

```
I  G  A  K  I  J  H  G  T  P  I  P  N  P  K  L
N  R  P  E  M  O  S  E  U  R  G  X  U  L  E  A
J  O  B  R  I  W  K  Z  O  V  Z  R  M  E  W  T
Q  T  X  T  O  G  P  Y  J  D  T  P  U  D  V  N
L  E  Z  N  E  C  H  C  B  O  I  C  A  G  X  E
G  S  C  E  B  O  R  H  W  R  L  R  I  E  Z  U
P  Q  H  N  X  R  X  A  G  Z  I  E  J  E  W  L
Z  U  O  I  R  U  I  X  S  L  I  S  X  G  B  F
O  E  O  M  U  I  E  T  O  T  R  C  N  D  R  V
C  N  S  O  I  F  R  C  A  W  I  E  A  U  I  K
L  S  E  R  X  K  C  P  U  I  A  N  Z  R  T  A
I  D  Z  P  L  O  W  R  M  N  N  D  A  G  O  L
Q  X  F  Z  R  I  A  L  F  C  Z  O  L  T  N  G
U  A  Y  B  H  J  B  A  G  A  E  Y  N  L  E  P
E  R  N  P  R  O  C  E  S  S  I  O  N  I  B  F
Y  Q  N  W  N  K  G  N  V  T  D  A  B  J  C  H
```

Answers

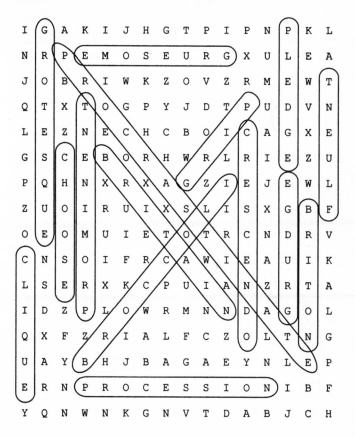

```
I  G  A  K  I  J  H  G  T  P  I  P  N  P  K  L
N  R  P  E  M  O  S  E  U  R  G  X  U  L  E  A
J  O  B  R  I  W  K  Z  O  V  Z  R  M  E  W  T
Q  T  X  T  O  G  P  Y  J  D  T  P  U  D  V  N
L  E  Z  N  E  C  H  C  B  O  I  C  A  G  X  E
G  S  C  E  B  O  R  H  W  R  L  R  I  E  Z  U
P  Q  H  N  X  R  X  A  G  Z  I  E  J  E  W  L
Z  U  O  I  R  U  I  X  S  L  I  S  X  G  B  F
O  E  O  M  U  I  E  T  O  T  R  C  N  D  R  V
C  N  S  O  I  F  R  C  A  W  I  E  A  U  I  K
L  S  E  R  X  K  C  P  U  I  A  N  Z  R  T  A
I  D  Z  P  L  O  W  R  M  N  N  D  A  G  O  L
Q  X  F  Z  R  I  A  L  F  C  Z  O  L  T  N  G
U  A  Y  B  H  J  B  A  G  A  E  Y  N  L  E  P
E  R  N  P  R  O  C  E  S  S  I  O  N  I  B  F
Y  Q  N  W  N  K  G  N  V  T  D  A  B  J  C  H
```

Break Dancing

Along with listening for blends, you can listen for syllables. A *syllable* is a single unit of sound including a vowel. Breaking a word into its parts can help you hear each part.

1-Syllable Word	*2-Syllable Word*	*3-Syllable Word*
nice	nice-ly	hos-pi-tal

4-Syllable Word	*5-Syllable Word*
ca-tas-tro-phe	u-ni-ver-si-ty

Divide and Conquer

Sort the following words according to the number of syllables they have.

reconnaissance	cache	vociferous	sleazy
evangelism	reign	technician	vein
particular	verbatim	conciliatory	vacuum
riskiness	rhythm	sociable	revile
subterranean	extravagant	apparently	approximately
seize	rhyme	unique	condominium
vacation			

Answers

1-Syllable Word	*2-Syllable Word*	*3-Syllable Word*
reign	revile	vacation
rhyme	rhythm	technician
vein	vacuum	riskiness

(Answers continued)

1-Syllable Word	2-Syllable Word	3-Syllable Word
seize	sleazy	sociable
cache	unique	verbatim

4-Syllable Word	5-Syllable Word
apparently	approximately
particular	conciliatory
reconnaissance	evangelism
extravagant	subterranean
vociferous	condominium

Cut to the Chase

Learning to spell consonant sounds, including /k/, /j/, /ch/, and blends can help you learn how to spell many everyday words. So can dividing a word into its consonants because that helps you hear each sound. Do a lot of word puzzles to get even more familiar with the quirks of English spelling. ▪

Chapter 8

Some Wicked Vowel
Movements

■ ■ ■

"Nothing you can't spell will ever work." — *Will Rogers*

See? It's really practical to know how to spell well.

English Spelling: Easy Words, Not-So-Easy Words, Totally Infuriating Words

As you've no doubt discovered through personal experience, English spelling has easy, middling, and challenging words. Here's why:

Easy Words

The easy words are based around one syllable and a sound that makes logical sense. You can make the word longer by adding prefixes and suffixes, but the root is visible and easy to decode. That makes the word a snap to spell. Here are some examples:

Easy Root	Add a Prefix	Add a Suffix
field	outfield	outfielder
frost	defrost	defrosted
stand	understand	understanding

Piece of cake. In many cases, just slice the words into their pieces and spell each piece.

Not-So-Easy Words

In some cases, these words pose bothersome spelling problems because they can't be reduced to one syllable. In other cases, not-so-easy words have entered English from other languages. As a result, these words have patterns we don't recognize. People brought up in Hong Kong, Tasmania, or Guam might know the words, but fat lot of good that does us. Embark on the following adventure to see what I mean.

Thorny Words

Underline the incorrectly spelled word in each line and correct it.

From French

1. chatoe	gauche	_____
2. mistique	hauteur	_____
3. bourgeois	raport	_____
4. ennui	insouceance	_____

From Spanish

5. barbequoo	pimento	_____
6. patio	tortila	_____
7. anchovie	vanilla	_____
8. avicado	marinade	_____

From Italian

9. bravo	artisen	_____
10. caricature	dillettante	_____
11. camoe	grotesque	_____
12. indigo	mezannine	_____

From Persian

13. assasin	pistachio	_____
14. bazaar	biege	_____
15. calender	serendipity	_____
16. kahki	zircon	_____
17. aubergine	suger	_____

From African languages

18. ardvark	merengue	_____
19. jamborie	voodoo	_____
20. aparthied	tsetse	_____

Answers: 1. chateau; 2. mystique; 3. rapport; 4. insouciance; 5. barbecue; 6. tortilla; 7. anchovy; 8. avocado; 9. artisan; 10. dilettante; 11. cameo; 12. mezzanine; 13. assassin; 14. beige; 15. calendar; 16. khaki; 17. sugar; 18. aardvark; 19. jamboree; 20. apartheid.

British English is not the same as American English. For instance, the British use "our" (as in *colour)* where Americans use "or" (as in *color).* The Brits also invert *er* at the end of a word. We spell *theater;* they spell *theatre.* There are other differences as well. On this side of the pond, always use American spelling.

In most cases, you can master these words by knowing their language of origin. This will help you familiarize yourself with the spelling patterns these words share, such as the French patterns *eaux* (as in *chateau)* and *ique* (as in *mystique).*

Totally Infuriating Words

Some words drive spellers to distraction because they don't make sense. Usually, they're not phonetic—they don't follow any of the patterns you learned in the previous chapters. As a result, they look incorrect even when they are correct. These words were just born to be bad. Unfortunately, they're often very useful.

Categorizing them according to the reason why they're difficult to spell can make them easier to grasp, however. Remember what you learned earlier in this book about grouping words with similar spelling patterns together. Grouping helps you visualize how to spell them. If you can't spell the exact word you want, you can often find one with the same pattern—the same silent letter, for instance—which will trigger your memory. Voila! You'll recall how to spell the word that you need. Let's take a look at some of these words now.

Here are some of my favorite totally infuriating words:

anonymous	appreciate	arithmetic
beggar	biscuit	bouquet
bureau	bursar	calendar
captain	celebrate	cellar
chamois	colonel	Connecticut
cylinder	electrician	delineate
fuchsia	hiccough	hideous
lieutenant	mansion	mountain
naive	paralysis	porcelain
privilege	revolution	seminar
sieve	sponsor	spontaneous
suite	surgeon	syllable
sympathy	symphony	synthesis
tyranny	villain	yacht

Spell each totally infuriating word correctly.

1. captin   _____
2. electrican   _____
3. burser   _____
4. porcelin   _____
5. Wedesday   _____
6. surgon   _____
7. fushia   _____
8. Conneticut   _____
9. sponser   _____
10. calender   _____

Answers: 1. captain; 2. electrician; 3. bursar; 4. porcelain; 5. Wednesday; 6. surgeon; 7. fuchsia; 8. Connecticut; 9. sponsor; 10. calendar.

Some Letters Should Be Seen but Not Heard

What do the words *subpoena, gnarled,* and *spaghetti* have in common? What about *muscle, knob,* and *almond?* They all have a silent letter, a bump in the sidewalk just waiting to trip you up.

William Shakespeare, no stranger to the peculiarities of English spelling, included this spelling rant in his play *Love's Labor's Lost:*

> I abhor such fanatical phantasms, such insociable and point-device companions; such rackers of orthography, as to speak dout, fine, when he should say dou*b*t; det, when he should pronounce de*b*t—d, e, b, t, not d, e, t; he clepeth a calf, cauf; half, hauf; neighbour vocatur nebour, neigh abbreviated ne. This is abhominable—it insinu-ateth me of insanie (5, 1).

Alas and alack, many useful English words have letters that we don't pronounce. Here are some hints for learning these busters:

1. Deliberately mispronounce the word, saying the silent letter. For instance, say **heir** instead of *air;* say crum**b** instead of *crum.* Of course, do this in your head, not aloud. Otherwise, people are likely to stare at you.

2. Group the words according to their silent letter. Put 'em in small packs of five or so, like sticks of chewing gum.

3. Practice the words. Write them as often as you can:
when it comes to spelling, familiarity breeds mastery,
not contempt. (Well, maybe you *will* grow to hate
these words, but tough noogies. You need them, you
really need them.)

Now, let's look at some of these honeys.

Words with Silent b, c, ch

English has many of these words, ladies and gentlemen,
which I've grouped in logical ways for your study pleasure.
Feel free to regroup them as you will. Use whatever groupings make the most sense to you because this'll help you
learn to spell the words more easily.

b	*c*	*ch*
Words with the *bt* pattern: debt, doubt, redoubtable, subtle	Words with the *cq* pattern: acquaint, acquit, acquire	bachelor, cheese, church, kitchen, peach, catch, watch, chore
Words with the *mb* pattern: plumber, tomb, lamb, climb, bomb, comb, crumb, dumb, numb, thumb	Words with the *sc* pattern: corpuscle, descend, muscle, scissors, fascinate, miscellaneous, scent, ascertain	chaise, chef, chiffon, cache, parachute, moustache, machine, brochure, chalet, champagne, chateau, chandelier, chaperone, brochure, Chopin

b	c	ch
	indict	Place names: Chicago, Michigan, Lake Champlain, Massachusetts
	czar	yacht

Words with Silent d, g, h

We pronounce *gn* in the following words: *signal, signature, resignation.* That said, here are some words where the silent letters remain silent:

d	g	h
handkerchief	Words with *eign* pattern: reign, foreigner	Words with *gh* pattern: light, caught
handsome	Words with *sign* pattern: sign, design, resign	heir, honor
Wednesday	diaphragm	Words with *wh* pattern: what, when, where, why
	campaign	Words with *hy* pattern: rhythm, rhyme

Words with Silent k, l, m

B can be silent, *m* can be silent, but in some words, *mb* is pronounced. This makes them easier to spell. Here are some examples: *bombard, combine,* and *crumble.* Similarly, the letters *mn* are pronounced in these words: *autumnal, hymnal,* and *solemnity.* Here are some words with a silent k, l, or m:

k	*l*	*m*
Silent *k* in the beginning of a word: knee, kneel, knelt, know, knew, known, knowledge, knife, knight, knot	Words with *lf:* calf, half	Mnemonic
Silent *k* in the middle of a word: asked	Words with *lm:* balm, calm, palm, psalm	
	Words with *lk:* chalk, talk, walk, folks	
	Words with *ld:* could, should, would	
	Words with *al:* almond, salmon colonel, salve	

Words with Silent n, p, s

Words with these silent letters fall into different categories, depending on the position of the letter in the word as well as the word's origin. For instance, the following words born in France but now living in America all have a silent *t*: *chalet, gourmet, depot, debut, crochet, ballet,* and *buffet.* Here are some additional words with a silent n, p, or s:

n	p	s
autumn	*p* at the beginning of a word: pneumonia, pseudonym, psychiatrist, psalm	aisle, island, debris
hymn	*p* in the middle of a word: corps, coup, cupboard, raspberry, receipt	State names: Arkansas, Illinois
solemn, column		

Words with Silent st, t, th, w

Here are some additional words with silent letters. Will these words never speak up?

s	t	th
Words with *sw:* answer, sword	Words with *st:* castle, whistle, chestnut, Christmas, fasten, listen	asthma, isthmus
	Words with *oft:* often, soften	With consonants before and after at the end of a word, the middle *th* is silent: clothes, months, depths, lengths
	With three consonants at the end of a word, the middle consonant (the *t*) is silent: acts, ducts, students	
	mortgage, catch, kitchen	

w

Words with *wh:* whole, who, whom, whose	Words with *wr:* write, wrote, written, writing, wrap, wrestle, wrist

---

Nome, Alaska, was misnamed because it was mis-spelled. A British cartographer wrote "Name?" in a map, as a request to clarify the region's name. The map's transcribers misinterpreted "name" as "Nome."

Give It a Shot

So many lists! Here's your reward: six jokes. Naturally, I'm going to make you choose the correct spelling of each word in parentheses.

1. *Question:* (Miscellaneous, Misellaneous) fact: Before Mount Everest was discovered, what was the highest mountain on Earth?

   Answer: Mount Everest

2. *Question:* I have no (doubt, dout) you know this one: What is the end of everything?

   Answer: The letter *g*.

3. *Question:* If you are a (bachelor, bacelor) in a dark (chateau, chatoo) with a candle, a woodstove, a match, and a gas lamp, which do you light first?

   Answer: The match

4. *Question:* There is a clerk at the butcher shop. He has (asthma, asma), he likes (almond, amond) cookies, and he works a double shift on (Wednesdays, Wenes-

days). He has a wife and two kids and wears a size 13 shoe. What does he weigh?

Answer: Meat.

5. *Question:* An airplane goes down on the border between the United States and Canada in a (rasberry, raspberry) patch. Where do they bury the survivors?

Answer: You don't bury survivors.

6. *Question:* Imagine that you are in a sinking rowboat surrounded by sharks. You can't reach the (iland, island). How would you survive?

Answer: Quit imagining!

Answers: 1. miscellaneous; 2. doubt; 3. bachelor, chateau; 4. asthma, almond, Wednesdays; 5. raspberry; 6. island.

Cut to the Chase

Learn challenging words by placing them in logical categories, such as country of origin or silent letters. Practice the words as often as you can. To catch silent letters, silently pronounce the word to yourself, saying *all* the letters. ▪

Chapter 9

What's with These Prefixes and Suffixes?

■ ■ ■

Question: Which English word has three consecutive double letters?
Answer Choices: Casseette? Tooffee? Tobbaacco? Book-keeper?

In this chapter, I'll explain how to add bits and pieces before and after base words so that you can figure out which letters are doubled—and which ones aren't. (By the way, the English word with three consecutive double letters is *bookkeeper.* But you figured that out already.)

Speed and Spell

You love it, you just love it—so here's a little more of it. Circle the ten misspelled words in the following joke. Then complete the list that follows.

A blonde's car gets a flat tire on the interstate one day. Not a foolharty sterotypical blonde, she carfully eases it over onto the shoulder of the road. She steps out of the car and opens the trunk. She takes out two cardboard men, assemmbles the few parts efficeintly, and stands them at the rear of the vehical facing oncoming traffic. The lifelike cardboard men are in trench coats exposeing their nude bodies to approaching drivers.

Not surprisingly, the traffic snarls and backs up. It isn't very long before a police car arrives. The officer, clearly enragged, asesses the situation and approaches the blonde of the disabled vehicle, yelling, "What is going on here?"

"My car broke down, officer," says the woman, calmly.

"Well, what are these obscene cardboard pictures doing here by the road?" asks the officer.

"Well," replies our heroine without the slightest bit of embarrasment, "those are my emergency flashers."

Misspelled Word	Corrected Word

Answers

Misspelled Word	*Corrected Word*
foolharty	foolhardy
sterotypical	stereotypical
carfully	carefully
efficeintly	efficiently
assemmbles	assembles
vehical	vehicle
exposeing	exposing
enragged	enraged
asesses	assesses
embarrasment	embarrassment

Now let's take a little drive down the highway of broken dreams. It's littered with the mangled remains of words with prefixes, suffixes, and double letters.

Google is an accidental misspelling of *googol.* According to Google's vice president, the Google's founders, well known for their poor grasp of spelling, registered *Google* as a trademark and web address before someone pointed out that it was spelled incorrectly.

Adding Prefixes

Words with double letters can be a speller's downfall. For example, how many times have you tripped on the words *recommended, embarrassed, underrated, accommodating, innocuous,* and *occurring?* Even the best spellers get sidetracked by these confounding words. In fact, one of the most commonly misspelled words of all is *misspelled!* Most of these problems arise from the "prefix," that pesky but useful letter or group of letters added to the front of a word to change its meaning.

A *prefix* is a letter or group of letters added to the beginning of a word to change its meaning.

Be still my beating heart—there's actually an easy way to figure out the correct spelling of many of these words:

Cool Rule

When a prefix is added to a word, the base word does not change. Don't add or subtract any letters.

Some words with prefixes that result in double letters:

Prefix	Base Word	New Word
im	mature	immature
ir	religious	irreligious
mis	shaped	misshapen
mis	step	misstep
under	rated	underrated

Remember: you don't drop or add a letter when a prefix is added. Here are some common spelling screwups:

Prefix	Base Word	Word Misspelled Because an Extra Letter Is Added
un	exceptional	uneexceptional
re	commended	reccommended
dis	integration	dissintegration
dis	appearance	dissappearance
dis	illusion	dissillusion

A *suffix* is a letter or group of letters added to the end of a word to change its meaning, tense, or part of speech.

Adding Suffixes

Now we enter the major leagues—adding suffixes. They're the same as prefixes—a letter or group of letters—but they're added to the end of a word rather than to the front. Suffixes do a lot more than prefixes too: they can change a word's meaning, tense, time, and part of speech. Here's how to deal with suffixes:

Types of Suffixes

Suffixes come in two flavors: those that begin with a vowel and those that begin with a consonant. Here are some examples:

Consonant Suffixes		Vowel Suffixes	
-cess	-ful	-able	-age
-hood	-less	-al	-ance

Consonant Suffixes		Vowel Suffixes	
-ly	-ment	-ant	-ar
-ness	-ry	-ing	-ish
-ty	-ward	-ist	-ism
-wise		-o	-on

Consonant suffixes are kindly souls; vowel suffixes not so much. As a result, spelling issues occur with vowel suffixes. It's always those pesky vowels, isn't it? (And don't come after me if you have a tender place in your breast for vowel suffixes. I've always preferred prefixes.) Here's how suffixes affect spelling:

Adding Suffixes That Start with a Consonant

Adding suffixes that start with a consonant is easy, as you'd expect.

Base Word	Suffix That Starts with a Consonant	Word with Suffix
peace	ful	peaceful
child	hood	childhood
age	less	ageless

When a base word ends in *y*, the *y* changes to *i* when a suffix is added. Here are some examples:

Word	Word with Suffix
body	bodily
happy	happiness

And here are some common exceptions. (Like you thought there wouldn't be any? Ha!):

ladylike	babyish	hurrying	dryly
dryness	shyly	spryness	miscellaneous

When a base word ends in a silent *e*, the *e* is kept before a suffix that starts with a consonant. Here are some examples:

Word	*Suffix That Starts with a Consonant*	*New Word Spelled Correctly*
care	ful	careful
excite	ment	excitement
fierce	ly	fiercely
sore	ly	sorely

Some exceptions: *argument, awfully, ninth, truly, wholly.* Notice that they're all important words, especially when you're writing *very truly yours* for the *ninth* (not nineth) time.

Ah, now to adding suffixes that start with a vowel. Gird your loins, ladies and gentlemen. (That's *lady* + *ies* = *ladies* and *gentle* + *men* = *gentlemen.*)

Adding Suffixes That Start with a Vowel

Just as you learned with suffixes that start with a consonant, when a base word ends in *y*, the *y* changes to *i* when a suffix is added. Here are some examples.

Word	*Word with Suffix*
puppy	puppies
vary	various

Double the final consonant of a word that ends with certain letters: *b, d, g, m, n, p, r, t.* This applies to the common suffixes that start with a vowel: *-ed, -ing, -er, -est.*

Base Word	*Last Letter on the Base Word*	*New Word*
rob	b	robbing, robbed, robber
sad	d	sadder, saddest
big	g	bigger, biggest
swim	m	swimming, swimmer
win	n	winning, winner
pop	p	popping, popped, popper
prefer	r	preferring, preferred
hit	t	hitting, hitter

Here's another way to look at this situation: the 1-1-1 rule. If you have one syllable, one consonant, and one vowel, double the final consonant before adding a suffix that begins with a vowel. For instance:

One-Syllable Word	*One Consonant*	*One Vowel*	*New Word*
bat	t	ed	batted
prod	d	ing	prodding

In words of more than one syllable, double the final consonant only when the final syllable is stressed.

Word with a Stressed Final Syllable	Word with an Unstressed Final Syllable
begin ➞ beginning	open ➞ opening
remit ➞ remittance	organ ➞ organize
defer ➞ deferring	offer ➞ offering

British English always doubles the final syllable when a suffix is added, whether or not the syllable is stressed. For example: the British spell it *travelled*; we spell it *traveled*.

Quick Stretch

Complete this chart by adding the suffixes to each base word:

Word	Suffix	New Word
1. many	fold	_____
2. marry	age	_____
3. fury	ous	_____
4. company	on	_____
5. beauty	ful	_____
6. dry	ness	_____

Answers

Word	Suffix	New Word Spelled Correctly
1. many	fold	manifold
2. marry	age	marriage
3. fury	ous	furious

(Answers continued)

Word	Suffix	New Word Spelled Correctly
4. company	on	companion
5. beauty	ful	beautiful
6. dry	ness	dryness

When a base word ends in silent *e,* the *e* is dropped before a suffix that begins with a vowel. Here are some examples:

Word	Suffix That Begins with a Vowel	New Word Spelled Correctly
fame	ous	famous
refuse	al	refusal
cure	able	curable
slice	ing	slicing
offense	ive	offensive

Stretch Again

Complete this list by adding the suffixes to each base word:

Word	Suffix	New Word Spelled Correctly
1. nose	y	_____
2. pole	al	_____
3. pure	ity	_____
4. convince	ing	_____
5. ice	icle	_____
6. defense	less	_____

Word	Suffix	New Word Spelled Correctly
7. awe	fully	_____
8. true	ly	_____
9. nine	ty	_____
10. disparage	ment	_____

Answers

1. nose	y	nosy
2. pole	al	polar
3. pure	ity	purity
4. convince	ing	convincing
5. ice	icle	icicle
6. defense	less	defenseless
7. awe	fully	awfully
8. true	ly	truly
9. nine	ty	ninety
10. disparage	ment	disparagement

If the word ends in *-ce* or *-ge* and the suffix begins with a vowel, *a, o,* or *u,* you have to reconsider keeping the *e.*

Words That End in -ce	Words That End in -ge	Words That End with Other Letters
peace ➤ peaceable	manage ➤ manageable	acre ➤ acreage
notice ➤ noticeable	courage ➤ courageous	hoe ➤ hoeing
	change ➤ changeable	mile ➤ mileage

The /sh/ sound before a vowel suffix is spelled *ti, si,* or *ci,* as these examples show:

/sh/ Spelled ti	/sh/ Spelled si	/sh/ Spelled ci
part ➤ partial	expel ➤ expulsion	music ➤ musician
vacate ➤ vacation		electric ➤ electrician
rate ➤ ratio		statistics ➤ statisticians

When a vowel suffix comes after /ee/, it's usually spelled with the letter i, as in these examples: *Indian, ingredient, obvious, zodiac, medium,* and *material.*

Words with Double Vowels

In keeping with my mission to have you group words with shared spelling patterns, I've arranged the following words according to their double letter. See how much easier this makes it to study them. Some of these words have prefixes and suffixes; others are compound words. Still others are just plain annoying.

Double e	Double o
sheepskin	bookworm
engineering	zoology
fricassee	school
gazetteer	balloonist
bookkeeper	spoonful

Words with Double Consonants

These words all have double consonants. Which words on this list do you use often? Which ones usually cause you to scratch your head in bafflement?

Double c	Double d	Double f	Double g
broccoli	address	daffodil	toboggan
accurate	Armageddon	toffee	exaggeration
tobacco	oddity	suffrage	aggressor

Double l	Double m	Double s	Double z
gorilla	grammar	cassette	embezzle
syllabus	immersed	assignment	fizzle
intellectual	comma	engrossed	mozzarella

Try It in Ink

Complete the following crossword puzzle to practice spelling words with double letters. This puzzle uses ten words. Choose from the following twelve words:

mayonnaise	barrel	chauffeur	tyrannical
molasses	weevil	cirrhosis	colossal
embarrassment	rabbi	Mississippian	zucchini

(puzzle on following page)

ACROSS

2 huge
5 Jewish religious leader
8 overbearing
9 person who lives in Mississippi

DOWN

1 shame
2 driver
3 oily yellow condiment
4 disease
6 long green squash
7 syrup

Answers

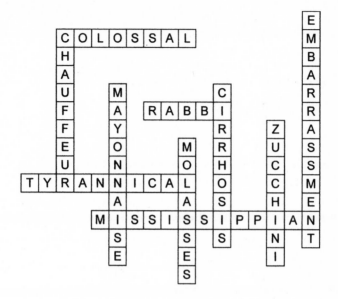

Cut to the Chase

Don't add or subtract any letters when you add a prefix to a root word. Suffixes, however, march to their own drummer. Be careful spelling words that have suffixes because they can be misleading, just like that man who invited you to his loft to see his etchings. ■

Chapter 10

Rule Your Vowel Movements

■ ■ ■

President Andrew Jackson stated, "It's a dam pur mind that can only think of one way to spell a word."

Well, he sure had no trouble, eh? What's with this *pur* stuff? In this chapter, I'll share some spelling rules that can help you learn how to spell the words you need only one way—the correct way.

For instance, in chapter 4 you learned:

I before *e*
Except after *c*
Or when sounded as *a*
As in *neighbor* and *weigh*

A good rule, that, but you also learned that a handful of words don't follow the rule. Since this is English spelling we're talking about, each rule does have some exceptions. And more exceptions. Nonetheless, having a starting place—a rule—does help you deal with a whole heap o' tricky spelling words.

Rule #1: Every Word Contains at Least One Vowel

Recall that the vowels are a, *e, i, o,* and *u.* The letter *y* is a pinch hitter, serving as both a vowel and a consonant. For example, it's a consonant in the word *yesterday* and a vowel in the word *shy.* Some languages form words without vowels—but English isn't one of them. Use this rule to help you remember how English words are constructed as you spell them.

And don't send me e-mail about abbreviations such as *km.* That's an abbreviation, not a word. And the word *psst*—now you're really reaching.

Rule #2: Every Syllable Contains One Vowel or Vowel Sound

As you learned earlier, a syllable is the smallest unit of a word. We have one-syllable words such as *at, are,* and *smack* and multisyllable words such as *pogrom* (two syllables: po/grom), *parallel* (three syllables: par/a/lel), *peninsula* (four syllables: pen/in/su/la), and so on. Use this rule to help you as you sound out words that are difficult to spell.

Rule #3: *q* Is Always Followed by a *u*

Nice rule because it has almost no exceptions. Here are some words that follow this rule:

iniquity	quality	quantum physics	quantity
quaff	quart	qualms	quake

quadrille	quadrant	quaint	quarantine
qualified	quark	quartz	quail
quarry	queen	query	queue
question	quetzal	quell	quench
quibble	quiescence	quietude	quick
quickly	quote	quotable	quota

Here are two exceptions: *Qiana* and *qwerty*.

Rule #4: If the Root Is a Complete Word, Add *-able,* and If the Root Isn't a Complete Word, Add *-ible*

- Acceptable or acceptible?
- Incredable or incredible?
- Desirable or desirible?

You learned the rule, so read the examples.

-able

-ible

Complete Word	New Word That Ends in -able	Words That End in -ible	
accept	acceptable	audible	incredible
advise	advisable	credible	indivisible
comfort	comfortable	crucible	inexpressible
depend	dependable	edible	legible
desire	desirable	eligible	negligible
excuse	excusable	fallible	permissible
fashion	fashionable	feasible	possible
laugh	laughable	horrible	terrible
value	valuable	inadmissible	visible

However, there are many exceptions. Here's a bunch:

accessible	collapsible	combustible	comprehensible
contemptible	convertible	defensible	digestible
discernible	forcible	reducible	responsible
	reversible	sensible	

As you noticed, if the root is a complete word ending in -*e*, drop the final -*e* and add the suffix.

You're It!

Complete each word with -*able* or -*ible*. (Naturally, try to get the one that's correct.)

1. accept_____
2. incorrupt_____
3. comfort_____
4. vis_____
5. desir_____
6. laugh_____
7. poss_____
8. fashion_____
9. excus_____
10. inexhaust_____
11. invinc_____
12. incorrig_____
13. irrepress_____
14. valu_____
15. ostens_____
16. plaus_____
17. compat_____
18. depend_____
19. gull_____
20. flex_____

Answers: 1. acceptable; 2. incorruptible; 3. comfortable; 4. visible; 5. desirable; 6. laughable; 7. possible; 8. fashionable; 9. excusable; 10. inexhaustible; 11. invincible; 12. incorrigible; 13. irrepressible; 14. valuable; 15. ostensible; 16. plausible; 17. compatible; 18. dependable; 19. gullible; 20. flexible.

Rule #5: *-cede* Is More Common Than *-ceed*

It's easy to remember how to spell the *seed* sound when the word refers to plant seeds. In that case, it's always spelled *s-e-e-d* as in *birdseed, cottonseed, flaxseed, linseed, poppyseed, pumpkinseed,* and so on. But what about the other seed sounds: *ceed, cede,* and *sede?*

When in doubt, choose *cede.* That's because only three English words end in *ceed: succeed, proceed,* and *exceed.* All the rest are spelled with *cede.* For instance:

accede	cede	concede	antecede
intercede	precede	recede	secede

And don't worry about *sede:* there's only one English verb that ends in *sede: supersede.*

Rule #6: The Ending *-cian* Always Refers to a Person, but *-tion* and *-sion* Are Never Used for People

The syllable at the end of *musician* and *condition* sound identical, but not so fast—*cian* always means a person, but *-tion* or *-sion* are never used for people. For instance:

Words That End in -cian	Words That End in -tion	Words That End in -sion
beautician	attention	compassion
electrician	attraction	concussion
magician	concentration	depression
mathematician	cooperation	discussion
obstetrician	corporation	expression

Words That End in -cian	Words That End in -tion	Words That End in -sion
optician	detection	obsession
pediatrician	detention	oppression
physician	intention	possession
statistician	integration	recession
technician	seduction	succession

In general, if the root word ends in /t/, use *-tion,* as in *complete, completion.* If the root word ends in /s/ or /d/, use *-sion* as in *extend, extension.* Naturally, there are exceptions, such as *permit/permission, submit/submission, omit/omission,* and *commit/commission.*

Suspicion and *ocean* don't fit any part of this rule. You're surprised there are exceptions?

Is it *-el* or *-le?* There's no rule, but *-le* is more common than *-el.* On the *-le* side we get *axle, battle, bottle, tackle, tickle, single, double,* and *triple.* On the *-el* side we get *angel, bushel,* and *parcel.* Words that end in *-il* are rare. *Civil* comes to mind.

Humorous Headlines

Circle the correct word in each set of parentheses in these ten actual advertisements:

1. For Sale by Owner: Complete set of *Encyclopedia Britannica.* 45 volumes. Excellent condition. $1,000.00 or best offer. Very (valuable, valuible) but no longer

needed. Got married last weekend. Wife knows everything.

2. Exercise (equipment, eqipment): queen-size mattress and box spring—$175.

3. Tired of working for only $9.75 per hour? We offer profit sharing and (flexible, flexable) hours. Starting pay: $7–$9 per hour.

4. Nice parachute. Never opened. High (quality, qality). Used once. Slightly stained.

5. (Attention, Attension): to person or persons who took the large pumpkin on Highway 87 near Harvey's Halloween (Attraction, Attracian). Please return the pumpkin and be checked. Pumpkin may be radioactive. All other plants in vicinity are dead.

6. (Incredible, Incredable) offer: Tickle Me Elmo, still in box, comes with its own 1988 Mustang, 51, auto, excellent condition $6,800.

7. (Desirable, Desirible) German shepherd. 85 lbs. Neutered. Speaks German. Free.

8. (Fashionable, Fashionible) '83 Toyota hunchback—$2,000.

9. *Star Wars*'s Job of the Hut—$15. (Quick, Qick) sale.

10. For sale by (statistician, statisticion). American flag. Sixty stars. Pole included. $100.

C says /s/ before an e, i, or y, as in *celebrate, celestial, cemetery, city,* and *cycle.* It says /k/ before everything else, as in *calendar, calisthenics,* and *callous.*

Answers: 1. valuable; 2. equipment; 3. flexible; 4. quality; 5. Attention, Attraction; 6. Incredible; 7. Desirable; 8. Fashionable; 9. Quick; 10. statistician.

Always capitalize proper nouns, words that name a specific person, place, thing, or idea.

Rule #7: Use *-ist* to Show "Someone Who Does Something" and Use *-est* for Superlative Adjectives

Words that end in *-ist* and *-est* sound alike, but don't be fooled. Here are some examples:

Words That End in -ist	*Words That End in -est*
dentist	finest
artist	sweetest
machinist	shortest

Rule #8: Words That End in *-ary* Are More Common Than Words That End in *-ery*

There's no rule here, but only six common words end in *-ery* rather than *-ary*. They are as follows:

cemetery	confectionery	distillery
millinery	monastery	stationery

Try It in Ink

Complete the following crossword puzzle to practice spelling the words in this chapter. This puzzle uses ten words. Choose from the following twelve words:

iniquity	monastery	queue	legible
sensible	mathematician	laughable	concede
physician	concussion	corporation	cemetery

ACROSS

5 line
8 company or a business
9 logical
10 wickedness, sin

DOWN

1 burial ground
2 humorous
3 easily read
4 medical doctor
6 head injury
7 give in

Answers

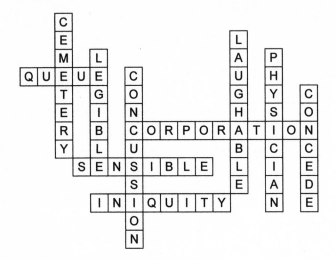

Cut to the Chase

Every word contains at least one vowel. Every syllable contains one vowel or vowel sound. *Q* is always followed by a *u*. If the root is a complete word, add *-able*. If the root isn't a complete word, add *-ible*. Words with *cede* are more common than words with *ceed*. The ending *-cian* always refers to a person; *-tion* and *-sion* are never used for people. Use *-ist* to show "someone who does something." Use *-est* for superlative adjectives. Always floss. ▪

Chapter 11

Tight Vowel Movements: Spelling Contractions and Plurals

■ ■ ■

Spelling is a lot like dating:

- Both can be fun.
- Both can be rewarding.
- Both can be disastrous.

And whether you're spelling or dating, first impressions count. Screw up on the first date, and you'll have to do a lot of damage control to get a second chance at love. Similarly, spell a crucial word wrong on a crucial document and people will think you're sloppy, or even worse—uneducated.

To review:

Spelling = dating.
First impressions matter.
Spell all the words in your personal ads correctly.

Let's try it now.

Personal Spelling

Read the following five personal ads. Then choose the correct spelling of each word in parentheses.

1. If you write to me, I promise that I (won't, wont) stalk you. Well, maybe just a little. I enjoy the (monkeys, monkies) in the zoo, reruns of *The Simpsons*, over-priced coffee, and running screaming through the rain. If (your, you're) not my ex-husband, an ax murderer, or the guy I saw peering into my window last Tuesday, contact me at hotmama428.gmail.

2. Retired photographer waiting to see what develops with you in a darkroom. I want a life where we'll sit on (benches, benchs) at the beach like bookends. I promise early-bird specials with discount coupons. If you feel the same way, (we're, were) made for each other. Male, nonsmoker, independently wealthy, a young 97.

3. Perennial Ph.D. candidate currently in his 17th year in the program, seeks independently wealthy woman. Age no barrier. Appearance no barrier, but must have all your own (teeth, teeths, tooths). You bring standing rib roast and (knives, knifes). I pay no (tax, taxes) and raise (wolves, wolfs). No photo necessary.

4. Single atheist white man, 54, seeking someone who lives in nearby (cities, citys). Any gender acceptable. Passionately interested in politics, hard-boiled eggs, Gregorian chants, telescopes, and limbo dancing.

Romanian-born, Texas-raised, former child star. Love is strange; but hey, you never know.

5. Divorced woman seeking someone who values joy, truth, beauty, justice, and me. Must be able to toast (bialys, bialies), mash (potatoes, potatos), and grow (tomatoes, tomatos). Drop it all to take frequent (journies, journeys) to North and South Poles on a moment's notice. Only tolerant men need to apply.

Answers: 1. won't, Monkeys; 2. benches, we're; 3. teeth, knives, taxes, wolves; 4. cities; 5. bialys, potatoes, tomatoes, journeys.

In these ads, I focused on two different types of spelling errors: contractions and plurals. They're the topic of this chapter, so let's straighten out these pesky vowel movements now.

Spelling Contractions

A *contraction* is a shorter form of two words. One of the words is always a verb, while the other can be a pronoun, verb, or other part of speech. An apostrophe (that odd mark of punctuation that looks like a comma in the air) is inserted in the spot where the letter or letters have been taken out. For example:

One letter removed	are	+	n*o*t	=	aren't
Two letters removed	I	+	*wi*ll	=	I'll

The following charts show some of the most useful contractions:

Pronoun + Verb Contractions

Pronoun	+	Verb	=	Contraction
I		would		I'd
I		had		I'd
I		will		I'll
I		am		I'm
I		have		I've
she		would		she'd
she		had		she'd
she		will		she'll
she		is		she's
she		has		she's
he		would		he'd
he		will		he'll
it		will		it'll
it		is		it's
it		has		it's
they		will		they'll
they		are		they're
they		have		they've
we		would		we'd
we		will		we'll
we		are		we're
we		have		we've
you		will		you'll
you		would		you'd
you		have		you've
you		are		you're
who		will		who'll

Verb + Not Contractions

Verb	+	Not	=	Contraction
are		not		aren't
can		not		can't
could		not		couldn't
did		not		didn't
does		not		doesn't
do		not		don't
had		not		hadn't
has		not		hasn't
have		not		haven't
is		not		isn't
must		not		mustn't
should		not		shouldn't
was		not		wasn't
were		not		weren't
will		not		won't
would		not		wouldn't

Notice that *won't* is a goofball: *will + not = won't*, not *willn't.* Go figure.

Word + Is Contractions

Word	+	Is	=	Contraction
here		is		here's
that		is		that's
there		is		there's
what		is		what's
where		is		where's
who		is		who's

Don't confuse the contraction *he'll* with *heal* or *heel*. Similarly, don't confuse the contraction *I'll* with the nouns *aisle/isle* or the contraction *we'd* with the word *weed*.

Mother Knows Best

Throughout the centuries, mothers have given their children plenty of good advice. The following is just a small sampling. Make each of the underlined phrases into a contraction. And don't forget to take the advice to heart:

_____ 1. Paul Revere's mother: "I <u>do not</u> care where you think you have to go, young man. Midnight is past your curfew."

_____ 2. Mona Lisa's mother: "After all that money your father and I spent on braces, Mona, <u>that is</u> the biggest smile you can give us?"

_____ 3. Humpty Dumpty's mother: "Humpty, if <u>I
   have</u> told you once, <u>I have</u> told you a
   hundred times not to sit on that wall. But
   would you listen to me? No."

_____ 4. Columbus's mother: "I <u>do not</u> care what
   <u>you have</u> discovered, Christopher. You
   still could have written."

_____ 5. Michelangelo's mother: "Mike, <u>cannot</u> you
   paint on walls like other children? Do you
   have any idea how hard it is to get that
   stuff off the ceiling?"

_____ 6. Napoleon's mother: "All right, Napoleon.
   If you <u>are not</u> hiding your report card
   inside your jacket, then take your hand
   out of there and prove it."

_____ 7. Barney's mother: "I realize strained plums
   are your favorite, Barney, but <u>you are</u>
   starting to look a little purple."

_____ 8. Batman's mother: <u>"It is</u> a nice car, Bruce,
   but do you realize how much the
   insurance is going to be?"

_____ 9. Mary's mother: <u>"I am</u> not upset that your
   lamb followed you to school, Mary, but <u>I
   would</u> like to know how he got a better
   grade than you."

_____ 10. Superman's mother: "Clark, your father
and I have discussed it, and <u>we have</u>
decided you can have your own cell
phone. Now will you quit spending so
much time in all those phone booths?"

Answers: 1. don't; 2. that's; 3. I've; 4. don't, you've; 5. can't;
6. aren't; 7. you're; 8. it's; 9. I'm, I'd; 10. we've.

**Some spelling errors are merely proofreading errors.
Find the spelling errors in these advertisements:**

1. **Ground beast: 99 cents per lb.**
2. **Kellogg's Pot Tarts: $1.99 box**
3. **Soft and genital bath tissues or facial tissue:
   89 cents**

Answers: 1. beef; 2. Pop-Tarts; 3. gentle

Are You Lonesome Tonight?

Read the following personal advertisements. Then find and
correct the errors in the contractions. Each advertisement
has multiple errors.

1. ALL CATS ARE GRAY IN THE DARK
   Female, 1922, some wear-and-tear but cleans up well.
   Hasnt many teeth but has a good upper plate and
   knee replacement. Is'nt in running condition, but
   walks well.

2. FRANK SINATRA OR PERRY COMO?
   Im still groovy, enjoy going 15 miles an hour in my

Prius on Thursday afternoons on the way to a few hands of Pinochle. Does a mean fox-trot and knows the difference between Manischewitz and Gallo wines. If youre a good cook, lets get together and cook up some brisket and kugel as we watch reruns of *Perry Mason.*

3. REMEMBER WHEN

If you remember when you had to adjust the rabbit ears on the television, when comics cost 12¢, and when the first man landed on the moon, you might remember when a man knew how to treat a woman like a lady. Meet me and let me show you. Its' worth a shot.

4. QUIET AT LAST

Im into privacy, short strolls, rainbows, the shallow end of the pool, diet soda, and contemplation. If your the silent type, lets get together, take our hearing aids out, and enjoy the peace and quiet.

5. PERMANENT RELATIONSHIP: BOCA

New widow—Ive just buried sixth husband—and seeking someone to round out the bridge table. Pacemaker, palpitations, blue-tinged skin wont be an issue.

Answers: 1. hasn't, isn't; 2. I'm, you're, let's; 3. it's; 4. I'm, you're, let's; 5. I've, won't.

Spelling Plurals

Remember that *singular* means one; *plural* means more than one. For instance:

Singular	*Plural*
one beetle	a forest infested with beetles
one noodle	a plate of noodles
one otter	an ocean filled with otters
one gimmick	too many gimmicks

Most English nouns spell their plural by simply adding a final -*s*. Notice that word *most*. Yes, there are more than a few nouns in English that form irregular plurals. They can be beasts. Let's tame them together.

Forming Regular Plurals

To form the plural of most words, just add an -*s* at the end, as the following examples show:

Singular Word	*Add -s to Form the Plural*	*Plural Word*
umbrella	⟶	umbrellas
zeppelin	⟶	zeppelins
zealot	⟶	zealots
vegetable	⟶	vegetables
vacuum	⟶	vacuums

Add -*es* if the noun ends in -*ch*, -*s*, -*sh*, -*x*, -*z*.

Word Ending	*Singular Word*	*Plural Word*
word ending in -ch	switch	switches
word ending in -s	glass	glasses
word ending in -sh	bush	bushes
word ending in -x	box	boxes
word ending in -z	buzz	buzzes

Forming Plurals with Nouns That End in -o

If the noun ends in vowel o (-ao, -eo, -io, -oo, -uo), add -*s*.

Word Ending Vowel + o	*Add -s to Form the Plural*	*Plural Word*
kangaroo	⟶	kangaroos
zoo	⟶	zoos
duo	⟶	duos
radio	⟶	radios
studio	⟶	studios

All musical terms ending in -*s* have plurals ending in just -*s*, as in *altos*, *cellos*, and *solos*.

If the noun ends in consonant o, add -*s* or -*es* or either one. (Yes, you get to spell the word two different ways and still be correct. When it comes to spelling, take what pitiful rewards you can.)

Word Ending Consonant + o	*Ending*	*Plural Word*
armadillo	-s	armadillos
casino	-s	casinos
gazebo	-s	gazebos
potato	-es	potatoes
echo	-es	echoes
hero	-es	heroes
buffalo	either -s or -es is acceptable	buffalos, buffaloes
cargo	either -s or -es is acceptable	cargos, cargoes

Word Ending Consonant + o	Ending	Plural Word
avocado	either -s or -es is acceptable	avocados, avocadoes
volcano	either -s or -es is acceptable	volcanos, volcanoes

The More, the Merrier

Form the plurals of these ten words. You may have to consult a dictionary.

Singular Word	Plural Word
1. embargo	_____
2. tomato	_____
3. typo	_____
4. echo	_____
5. veto	_____
6. domino	_____
7. grotto	_____
8. auto	_____
9. innuendo	_____
10. soprano	_____

Answers: 1. embargoes; 2. tomatoes; 3. typos; 4. echoes; 5. vetoes; 6. dominos, dominoes; 7. grottoes, grottos; 8. autos; 9. innuendo, innuendoes; 10. sopranos.

Forming Plurals with Nouns That End in -y

If the noun ends in consonant -*y*, change the -*y to -i* and add -es.

Word Ending Consonant + y	Ending	Plural Word
baby	-es	babies
spy	-es	spies
poppy	-es	poppies
blackberry	-es	blackberries
lady	-es	ladies

If the noun ends in vowel + *y*, just add -s.

Word Ending Vowel + y	Ending	Plural Word
attorney	-s	attorneys
day	-s	days
delay	-s	delays
survey	-s	surveys
toy	-s	toys
honey	-s	honeys

Forming Plurals with Nouns That End in -f or -fe

Many—but not all—of these words just get an -s. Some change the *f* to *v* and then get an *-es*. Sadly, there's no rule: the plural of these words is maddeningly random.

Word Ending -f or -fe	Ending	Plural Word
belief	-s	beliefs
chief	-s	chiefs
staff	-s	staffs
knife	change the f to v and add -es	knives

Word Ending -f or -fe	Ending	Plural Word
thief	change the f to v and add -es	thieves
wife	change the f to v and add -es	wives

Forming Plurals with Nouns That Are Cranky

Some nouns change their spelling when they become plural. Why? Just to vex us. Here are some common and useful examples:

Singular	Plural
man	men
woman	women
child	children
foot	feet
goose	geese
mouse	mice

Other nouns have the same form whether they're singular or plural. These include:

Singular	Plural
deer	deer
moose	moose
series	series
sheep	sheep
species	species

These nouns are plural but do not end in -s: *people*, *police*, and *cattle.*

The following words have unusual plural forms because of their origin:

Singular	*Plural*
alumnus	alumni
analysis	analyses
antenna	antennae/antennas
appendix	appendices/appendixes
axis	axes
bacterium	bacteria
basis	bases
beau	beaux/beaus
corpus	corpora/corpuses
crisis	crises
criterion	criteria
curriculum	curricula
datum	data
diagnosis	diagnoses
focus	foci/focuses
fungus	fungi/funguses
hypothesis	hypotheses
index	indices/indexes
louse	lice
matrixes	matrices
mediums	media

Singular	*Plural*
nucleus	nuclei
parenthesis	parentheses
phenomenon	phenomena
radius	radii
stimulus	stimuli
stratum	strata
synopsis	synopses
thesis	theses

A Puzzle of Plurals

Complete the following crossword puzzle to practice spelling the plurals of the words you just learned.

ACROSS

1 the plural of zoo
3 the plural of tray
6 the plural of wolf
8 the plural of dictionary
9 the plural of monkey
10 the plural of valley

DOWN

2 the plural of spy
4 the plural of alumnus
5 the plural of tomato
7 the plural of child

Answers

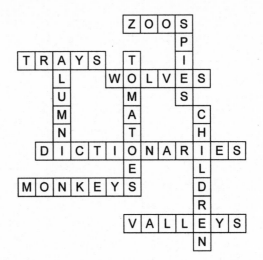

Cut to the Chase

A *contraction* is a shorter form of two words. An apostrophe is inserted in the spot where the letter or letters have been taken out. To form regular plurals, add an *-s* at the end of the noun. To form irregular plurals, follow the rules, hope for the best, and check your dictionary. ▨

Chapter 12

The Big Payoff

■ ■ ■

Several years ago, I had a devil worshipper in class who decided to deface a huge boulder outside the school. It took him several hours overnight to do the deed, but it was sure worth the time for us teachers. Why? The next morning we discovered that our naughty boy had painted "Satin Lives" in letters five feet high. Yes, the poor deluded child was declaring his allegiance to a fabric rather than a fiend. Moments like this make the sacrifices of being a teacher so worthwhile.

Why Are Some Words So Hard to Spell?

Okay, some words *are* more difficult to spell than others. Why? We've been down this road before, ladies and gentlemen. You learned that some of these so-called spelling demons don't follow the rules. Others don't look right, even when they are. Many are easily confused with other words. A few have poor personal hygiene and shaky interpersonal skills, but we'll ignore them.

Whatever the reason, these spelling demons are among

the most often used words in English, so let me help you master some of them.

Twenty Common Spelling Demons:
All Nouns That Identify People

You know that grouping words by common qualities can make them easier to learn, so here are twenty nouns that all name people. Read the list and spell the words using the techniques that you learned in chapter 4.

alumna	amateur	assassin	bachelor
ballerina	benefactor	buccaneer	burglar
celebrity	chauffeur	chief	colleague
colonel	concierge	connoisseur	deacon
friend	genius	mathematician	principal

Solve the Puzzle

Complete the following crossword puzzle to practice spelling the nouns that identify people who you just learned. This puzzle has ten words.

ACROSS

7 dancer
8 mnmarried man
9 thief
10 religious leader

DOWN

1 driver
2 military rank
3 famous person
4 co-worker
5 hired killer
6 not a professional

Answers

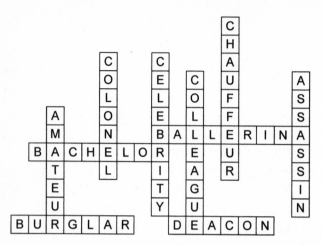

Twenty More Common Spelling Demons:
All Nouns That Identify People

Twenty more words about people, my friends. Why not add these to your word cards?

psychologist	niece	orphan	notary
guardian	rogue	linguist	patriot
rookie	quack	raconteur	peer
picador	playwright	premier	president
minor	miner	marquis	mercenary

Twenty Common Spelling Demons:
All Nouns That Name Places

We'll go from people to places. You'll see that some of these words are proper nouns, so be sure to capitalize them when you spell them.

building	business	parliament	capitol
Mediterranean	Albuquerque	bazaar	Caribbean
Britain	cafeteria	California	carnival
cemetery	condominium	Connecticut	laboratory
labyrinth	lavatory	restaurant	suite

Check and Double-Check

Circle the six misspelled words in the following headlines and complete the list that follows. (Yes, these are actual headlines. I didn't make them up.)

1. Some 40 percent of female gas station employees in Califronia are women, up from almost none a year ago.

2. Publicize your restarant business absolutely free! Send $6.

3. Labaratory petroleum jelly keeps idle tools rust-free.

4. Britian's company makes offer to screw company stockholders.

5. Albaquerque governor offers rare opportunity to goose hunters.

6. Marijuana issue sent to a joint bussiness committee.

Misspelled Word	*Corrected Word*
1. _____	_____
2. _____	_____
3. _____	_____
4. _____	_____
5. _____	_____
6. _____	_____

Answers

1. Califronia	California
2. restarant	restaurant
3. labaratory	laboratory
4. Britian's	Britain's
5. Albaquerque	Albuquerque
6. bussiness	business

Twenty Common Spelling Demons: All Nouns That Name Things

The following twenty handy words all identify objects. Why not divide these words into syllables as you learn them?

argument	bureau	yacht	cellophane
chaos	criticism	committee	sponge
aperitif	antique	asterisk	statue
athlete	avalanche	babushka	umbrella
badminton	balloon	bicycle	ukulele

Hot Date

Read the following personal ads. Then choose the correct spelling of each word in parentheses.

1. Amana washer $100. Owned by clean bachelor with a (bicycle, bicicle) who seldom washed.

2. Full-sized mattress. Twenty-yr.-warranty. Like new, still in (cellophane, cellofane). Slight urine smell.

3. Free (badminton, badmitton) set with purchase of 3-bedroom, 2-bath home.

4. Joining nudist colony, must sell (burueau, bureau) and washer and dryer. $300.

5. (Antique, antiqe) snowblower for sale—only used on snowy days.

Answers: 1. bicycle; 2. cellophane; 3. badminton; 4. bureau; 5. Antique.

Stupid spelling joke:

Q: What comes once in a minute, twice in a moment, but not once in a thousand years?
A: The letter *m.*

Twenty Common Spelling Demons:
Words That Name Foods

Now we have twenty words about things we eat. To make these words easier to learn, create your own mnemonic (memory) devices, such as songs, chants, and rhymes.

banana	bouillon	cantaloupe	cocoa
saccharin	macaroon	raspberry	torte
barbecue	broccoli	champagne	lettuce
bologna	bouillabaisse	chocolate	zucchini

Here are six bonus words for fun. What a dreadful dish they'd make all served together.

salmon	sandwich	sauerkraut
spaghetti	pimento	ravioli

Dinner's On

Read these jokes. Then circle the six misspelled words and complete the list that follows:

Joke #1

An elderly couple were killed in an accident and next thing they knew they were being shown around heaven by Saint Peter. "Here is your beachfront condo, and over there are the two golf courses and three swimming pools. If you need anything to drink, there is a bar on every block. Oh, and there's the barbecoo, champain fountain, and unlimited choclit area. They're all open 24/7."

"Heck, Gloria," the old man groaned when Saint Peter left them, "we could have been here ten years ago if you hadn't heard that show about those stupid high-fiber, low-fat, oat bran and samon diets!"

Joke #2

A lady was examining every single frozen turkey at the grocery store but couldn't find the right one for her large family. She grabbed some brocoli and letuce for the meal. Then she spotted a stock boy and asked, "Do these turkeys get any bigger?"

Looking surprised, he said, "No, ma'am; they're dead."

Misspelled Word	*Corrected Word*
1. _____	_____
2. _____	_____
3. _____	_____
4. _____	_____
5. _____	_____
6. _____	_____

Answers

1. barbecoo	barbecue
2. champain	champagne
3. choclit	chocolate
4. samon	salmon
5. brocoli	broccoli
6. letuce	lettuce

Twenty Common Spelling Demons:
Words That Describe People

Now we move from nouns to adjectives. These words can all be used to tell what people are like and how they act.

competent	courteous	efficient	dissatisfied
foreign	forty	fulfilled	irresistible
indispensable	transient	separate	unconscious
irrelevant	necessary	taciturn	arrogant
banal	berserk	conscientious	lackadaisical

Enough About You; Let's Talk About Me

Write the eight words from the preceding list that you would *most* like to have applied to you. Write each word twice.

1. _____   _____
2. _____   _____
3. _____   _____
4. _____   _____
5. _____   _____
6. _____   _____
7. _____   _____
8. _____   _____

Possible answers: 1. competent; 2. courteous; 3. efficient; 4. irresistible; 5. indispensable; 6. fulfilled; 7. conscientious; 8. necessary.

Now, write the eight words from the same list that you would *least* like to have applied to you. Write each word twice.

1. _____   _____
2. _____   _____
3. _____   _____
4. _____   _____
5. _____   _____
6. _____   _____
7. _____   _____
8. _____   _____

Possible answers: 1. irrelevant; 2. banal; 3. dissatisfied; 4. berserk; 5. arrogant; 6. lackadaisical; 7. unconscious; 8. transient.

These three tricky spelling words describe events: *accidental*, *appropriate*, and *semiannual*.

Twenty Common Spelling Demons: All Verbs

And now we come to words that describe actions. Create a scene in your mind with these spelling demons.

achieve	acquire	acknowledge	concede
aggravate	commemorate	embarrass	conceited
fascinate	alter	collaborate	referee
conceive	contradict	courteous	reign
rescue	gauge	harass	negotiate

Hunt and Peck

Choose the word that's misspelled in each line. Then correct it.

1. aquire	achieve	acknowledge
2. referree	reign	rescue
3. fascinate	gauge	harrass
4. concieve	commemorate	conceited
5. negotiate	contradict	agravate

Answers: 1. acquire; 2. referee; 3. harass; 4. conceive; 5. aggravate.

Cut to the Chase

Have fun learning to spell. ▨